2/2/67

To Maur,

Best Wishes
&
Many Malds

Kathleen E. W. Gallagher

Maureen Doherty
16 Wheatland St.
Peabody, Mass.

ROBERT KENNEDY IN NEW YORK

ROBERT KENNEDY IN NEW YORK

GERALD GARDNER

RANDOM HOUSE   NEW YORK

TO HARRIET

whose help made all

of it possible

Stone, bronze, stone, steel, stone, oakleaves, horses' heels
Over the paving.

And the flags. And the trumpets. And so many eagles.

How many? Count them. And such a press of people.

We hardly knew ourselves that day, or knew the City.

This is the way to the temple, and we so many crowding the way.

So many waiting, how many waiting? What did it matter, on
    such a day?

Are they coming? No, not yet. You can see some eagles.
    And hear the trumpets.

Here they come. Is he coming? . . .

There he is now!

—*Coriolan* by T. S. Eliot

CONTENTS

⊨×⊐

⊨×⊐

[*x*]

[*xi*]

August 26, 1964

Dear Mr. Kennedy:

You recently said that you were committed to keeping alive the idealism and enthusiasm that your brother brought into government. As one who had great affection for the late President, I would like to join you in that effort.

I note that today you have declared your candidacy for the office of Senator from the State of New York. It occurs to me that I might be of help.

Please call on me if you share that belief.

Sincerely,
Gerald Gardner

My brief note to the Attorney General didn't tell the entire story. In the summer of 1963 I had made a silent promise that when Jack Kennedy ran for re-election the following year, I would travel with that campaign train —as a writer, an aide, I knew not what—but I would be aboard.

This intention was not as unrealistic as it might seem. The previous fall a letter had reached me on the cool green stationery of the White House. Above an undecipherable signature were a few crisp paragraphs from the President.

He had enjoyed my book, *Who's in Charge Here?*, and would like me to visit him at the White House. That twenty-minute meeting in the beige oval office had led to others—on a series of books about America's unfinished business—with Schlesinger, Sorensen, Salinger, Heller, Weaver, and Robert F. Kennedy.

That first meeting with Robert Kennedy in the spring of 1963 was instructive. There were three of us in the Attorney General's outer office—Presidential aide Arthur Schlesinger, Jason Epstein of Random House, and myself. Kennedy's secretary had turned to Epstein and said, "The Attorney General will see you in a moment, Mr. Schlesinger . . ."

Robert Kennedy's office was immense. The diffident, shirt-sleeved fellow with the face of a worn teen-ager seemed at first to be dwarfed by it. The wounded smile on the bronzed face suggested vulnerability, but there was the hint of steel in the mouth and jaw. He sat there in an executive swivel chair that seemed to engulf him, and stared at us across a desk strewn with papers in seeming disarray. No less than six file baskets were arranged like massed battalions, each threatening to overflow with its burden of urgency.

Scotch-taped to the richly paneled wall behind him was an exhibit of finger painting by his children. On the far wall hung an enormous sailfish that I thought I had last seen in the Fish Room of the White House. Beneath it had been a plaque reading, "Caught by John F. Kennedy, January 1954."

"I see you took the fish from the Fish Room," I said.

"I did not," said the Attorney General with feeling. "I caught that fish."

During the meeting his multi-buttoned phone rang and he answered it. He was suddenly preoccupied, the meeting forgotten, our discussion far from his mind.

"I don't know," he said. "That *is* a problem. We'll have to do something about that. I think our best bet is to tell the children we'll take them riding *next* Sunday—"

The meeting bore fruit and a series of books—Ted Sorensen had suggested the title, "The New Frontier Series"—was in the works.

Then came November 22. And after that my focus had turned to the man who was closest to John Kennedy through the struggles of the early sixties, and the man to whom, for many at least, the torch had been passed.

Hence my letter to Robert Kennedy, offering to help in his campaign.

His answer came within forty-eight hours.

"Mr. Gardner?" said the competent female voice at the other end of the telephone.

"Yes."

"Mr. Robert Kennedy calling. One moment, please."

Then the voice I would hear so often in the weeks ahead.

"Hello. I have your letter and I'd like to take you up on that . . ."

ROBERT KENNEDY IN NEW YORK

CHAPTER 1

The Carlyle

The papers were full of the Kennedy invasion of New York. Some were infuriated, others delighted, none indifferent.

Robert Kennedy had suggested I meet him at his suite at the Carlyle Hotel, that elegant hostelry that had served as home and headquarters for President Kennedy on his frequent visits to New York City. Now it was home and headquarters to Robert Kennedy, as well as temporary home to Jacqueline Kennedy and her children while their Fifth Avenue apartment was being readied for occupancy.

It occurred to me, as I approached the front desk, that there were worse ways of disposing of the carpetbagger issue—which was already erupting against the candidate—than merely listing the mailing addresses of each of the Kennedy Klan. Bob at the Carlyle. Steve and Jean Kennedy Smith on Fifth Avenue in the Eighties. Joseph and Rose Kennedy on Central Park South. And the Kennedy family offices in the Pan Am Building on Park Avenue.

[3]

At the desk were two thirtyish men whose attire and mien bore the unmistakable stamp of advertising. They were asking for the Attorney General's suite and were told it was 11E. This spared me asking the same question, and I was turning to follow them to the bank of gilded elevators, when a youthful man, wearing a ruddy complexion and an oxford pin-stripe, crossed the lobby in strides that just bordered on a trot, turned a diffident face toward us, and said, "I'll be with you in a few minutes. You go on up." And then Robert Francis Kennedy disappeared through the revolving doors onto East 76th Street.

The living room of Suite 11E had something of the look of the oval office at 1700 Pennsylvania Avenue. It was furnished in beige, faultlessly though comfortably elegant. Perhaps it was this decorative kinship that satisfied the Kennedys with this home away from home.

The room was bursting with people. They all appeared bright, busy, and bushy-tailed—secretaries, press aides, speechwriters, advertising men, waiters bringing food and messengers bringing wires. They all seemed to be driven by a special dynamo.

In a few minutes Robert Kennedy returned. He stripped off his jacket and carelessly rolled up his sleeves, revealing a profusion of sandy-colored hair on his muscular forearms.

The two admen who had preceded me to the hotel desk—they were from Papert, Koenig & Lois, the advertising agency chosen to handle the Kennedy campaign—showed him the layout for a brochure proclaiming his candidacy and his chief virtues. He skimmed through it and pointed to a photo on page 4 that showed him shaking hands with some beaming dignitary beneath a headline trumpeting his ties to labor.

"There must be a better photo than this," he said.

"What's wrong with this one?" said the adman.

"That fellow's in jail," said the Attorney General.

No one was so impolite as to inquire whether Mr. Kennedy had put him there.

The other adman had spread out approximately two dozen eight-by-ten photographs of the Attorney General on the large coffee table. Bob Kennedy's closest aide, Ed Guthman, was busy discarding some by tossing them onto the sofa.

"Wait a minute," said Kennedy petulantly. "Why don't you clear those discards with me? Don't I have any say in the matter?"

"Sure, Bob," said Guthman, "but I didn't think you'd want to consider the ones where you're wearing a jacket. The shirt sleeves is more in your image."

"I don't know," said one of the admen. "My mother gets very exercised when she sees a picture of a senator without his jacket. She doesn't feel it's dignified."

The battle of the shirt sleeves was fought and won by the partisans of informality and the discarded photos remained in the oblivion of the sofa.

At this point I introduced myself.

"Oh yes," said the candidate. "Have you had a chance to look over my acceptance speech?"

The candidate had sent me a copy of the speech he planned to deliver before the Democratic State Convention.

"Yes, I think it's fine," I said.

A serious expression flashed across his face. "Do you think we should add some humor?" he said.

I told him I didn't think so.

He led the way out of the living room into one of the suite's three bedrooms. "Come on," he said, "I'll tell you a little about the campaign." I leaned back onto one of the beds as the candidate paced nervously by the window.

"Let me tell you some of my views on the problems of New York."

Then Robert Kennedy launched into a virtuoso performance on the ailments of the Empire State and its people. As I listened, my mind turned to the extemporaneous speech once delivered before the U.S. Chamber of Commerce by his older brother. President Kennedy had astonished his audience by reeling off a prodigious array of facts and figures on the economy.

Apparently Robert Kennedy's command of the facts —on education, housing, the needs of the elderly, the problems of the jobless and the young—was equally formidable. Even a Bobbyphobe, of which there was a growing number in the Empire State, would have to concede that the candidate had done his homework.

"Of course," he said, "it won't do for me to march into New York proclaiming the shocking, shameful state of affairs here. I'll have to take the position that New York is a great state, but it can be greater."

Again my thoughts returned to another Kennedy. No doubt early in the campaign of 1960 John Kennedy had paced another room and said, "It won't do for me to go about the United States proclaiming the shocking, shameful state of affairs. I'll have to take the position that America is a great country, but it can be greater . . ."

The parallels of the brothers' situations were numerous. Both were fighting against great initial difficulties. John Kennedy was young and he was Catholic. Robert Kennedy was reputedly ruthless, he was Massachusetts-born, and he opposed a popular incumbent.

The similarities in their appearance, manner, and voice were obvious, and those similarities carried with them an obvious advantage. Robert Kennedy had played a key role in his brother's administration, and the echo of his past struggles would surely impress his brother's admirers.

We rejoined the people in the living room. It was a new mix: some had left to be replaced by other bright, busy-looking people. The advertising men were still discussing the promotional brochure. The Attorney General joined them.

"I'm not sure about the slogan on the cover," he said as the agency men cringed. This was the slogan for the entire campaign and had doubtless evolved from dozens of searing brainstorming sessions. It would appear on banners, cards, signs, and billboards, many of which were probably already in production.

The slogan read, "Let's put Bob Kennedy to work for New York."

"It carries a built-in danger," said Kennedy. "It seems to me it emphasizes the very thing we want to *de*-emphasize—the fact that I come here from out of the state."

"However—" began the first adman.

[7]

"Nonetheless—" said the second adman.

"I think the rest is fine," said Bob Kennedy. "Now what about the photo for the cover? I don't think any of these are really satisfactory."

He was quite right. They made him resemble an administrative assistant reaching for a paper clip. One of the minor mysteries of the campaign was why not one piece of election paraphernalia, from the smallest lapel button to the largest banner, bore a photo of Robert F. Kennedy that was anything but grossly unflattering.

The agency men reluctantly agreed that the photos were less than they could be, but they pointed out that a quantity of the brochures was needed almost at once.

"Couldn't we print ten thousand with this photo," said the candidate, picking up the best of the lot, "then take a new photo and run the balance?"

"Sure," said the adman, his composure returning. "The expense of the ten-thousand run will be considerable, of course. But with the amount you'll be spending on this campaign, that shouldn't be a problem—"

"The hell it won't," snapped Kennedy. "That's the kind of thinking that can destroy you!"

He turned to his secretary. "Angie, get me Steve." Angie was Angie Novello, Robert Kennedy's patient, efficient secretary. Steve was Stephen Smith, Robert Kennedy's brisk, suave brother-in-law. Steve Smith had served Jack Kennedy in his campaign for the Presidency and Ted Kennedy in his campaign for the Senate. Now he was acting as Bob Kennedy's campaign manager. A man for all Kennedys, this Stephen Smith.

As the candidate outlined the problems of short runs

versus long runs and the deficiencies of the photographic art, a cautious-looking fellow in his mid-thirties strode into the room.

"Hello, Fred," said the admen with a blend of deference and regard that told me this must be their employer, Fred Papert, boy wonder of advertising and co-founder of Papert, Koenig & Lois.

Papert brought news of the agency's television plans. He perched on the edge of the sofa as his aides scooped up the discarded photos. Bob Kennedy returned to the group and straddled a chair opposite Papert as the others formed a parabola of chairs around them.

"We have some very exciting plans for television commercials," said Papert. "The basic aim of all our commercials, Bob, will be to present you as a warm, sincere individual."

Kennedy didn't break a smile. "You going to use a double?" he said.

The room exploded into laughter.

"Yes," said Papert. "That's the idea. You'll never once appear on camera. No, seriously, we're going to shoot you on actual locations—in rallies, at colleges, in supermarkets—surrounded by small crowds. People will ask you questions. You'll answer them. One-minute spots, three-minute spots, five-minute spots. Real excitement, real issues."

The idea was not without its appeal. At this stage no one could foresee that the one element of the idea that was unrealistic was the reference to "small crowds." Robert Kennedy never drew a small crowd from one end of the campaign to the other.

He was mobbed and shoved and kissed and dragged from the tops of cars. He was hugged by men and clawed by women. Let him come to a town of ten thousand and half that number would turn out. Let him arrive five hours late and the crowd had tripled. Let him merely walk down a street and a throng encircled him.

So two days before the Democratic State Convention, with a bruising campaign stretching out before them, a handful of men sat in an uptown hotel room discussing the merits of photographs and slogans, the formula for a TV commercial, the needs of the people of New York.

Here was the nucleus of the "well-oiled Kennedy machine" that had invaded New York to put Robert Francis Kennedy into the Senate of the United States.

CHAPTER 2

◄✕►

The Convention

The next day the Republican State Convention met to nominate Kenneth B. Keating for Senator. It was an interesting event. A lawyer from Nebraska made the nominating speech, a politician from Michigan seconded it, and a Congresswoman from Connecticut said a few words. And all they seemed able to agree upon was that carpetbagging was a shameful practice.

At the Carlyle, the candidate handed me a draft of his second campaign speech. It was to be delivered two days hence before the AFL-CIO and it carried a burden of some importance. For the union leaders were undecided whether to endorse Kennedy or to endorse no one. The latter course might be more prudent. For Keating's voting record on labor legislation had been sound, and no union opposes "a friend of labor"—especially if the friend is a popular incumbent who is likely to retain his seat.

So if Robert Kennedy was to receive the endorsement of the AFL-CIO it would be because the convention delegates responded overwhelmingly to his presence.

[*11*]

But the speech was not a speech. In its present form it had all the idealism and rhetoric of a legal brief. I retired to a back bedroom and started rewriting from the top.

When I had the new draft ready, the candidate took it into his bedroom and read it through at his usual headlong pace. Speed-reading seemed to be one more quality that the brothers Kennedy shared.

"I'd like to use this segment from page five in my acceptance speech. See if we can work it in."

Debs Myers, Kennedy's Salinger-shaped, cigar-smoking press secretary, entered the room.

"The *New York Times* put it to you again this morning," said Myers, worrying his cigar. "I've arranged for you to have lunch with a few of their editors."

"Do you think it will help?" said the candidate.

"Stranger things have happened."

"You think they'll endorse Keating?"

"Yes," said Myers.

"Their editorial said today that I was the best Attorney General in twenty years—and that I should stay there."

"I don't think the bastards like you," said Myers.

"Well, at least," said the candidate, "they can never say I got my job through the *New York Times*."

The following morning—the day the Democratic party would offer Bob Kennedy their nomination—I arrived at Suite 11E. I walked into the living room and was about to deposit my attaché case on the onyx coffee table, when Robert Kennedy gestured toward a deeply suntanned woman in a green silk dress.

"Ethel, this is Gerald Gardner."

Ethel Skakel Kennedy's face lit up and her hand darted out. "Oh, you are such a funny man. How wonderful to meet you." When she spoke her whole face came alive, making it impossible to doubt either her enthusiasm or her sincerity. A valuable woman for any candidate—or for any man.

Once again the living room was alive with activity. Angie Novello was noisily clacking away at a typewriter that rendered the acceptance speech in jumbo type onto sheets that would be inserted in the binder from which the candidate would deliver it in a few hours.

Ed Guthman was dispatching tomorrow's labor speech to press headquarters downtown at the Chatham Hotel, where it would be mimeographed and rushed to the press for tomorrow's editions.

The television set in the corner was ablaze with convention sounds from the National Guard armory on Park Avenue. From time to time Robert Wagner and Averell Harriman popped on the screen and spoke laudatory words on the subject of Robert Kennedy, the hope of New York.

Through all this, the hope of New York stood in the center of the living room, coolly assessing the events on the TV screen, a white bath towel wrapped around his middle. A mat of hair covered his muscular chest and it occurred to me that the candidate was in excellent condition. Just how well that condition was to serve him became apparent within the first taxing week of what must certainly rank as the most physically demanding campaign in a long, long time.

Suddenly the screen erupted with noise as a group of demonstrators captured a portion of the convention floor and paraded around and around in a tight little circle. Poor television reception made it difficult to identify the demonstrators' advocacy—were they for Kennedy or for Sam Stratton, a New York Assemblyman who was contesting the nomination?

"It's a Kennedy demonstration," said an aide. Kennedy looked dubious, and soon the announcer identified it as a demonstration for Mr. Stratton.

The candidate smiled. "I knew it couldn't have been mine. Much too small and poorly organized."

At this point the corridor door burst open with the suddenness of a gas-main explosion and a troup of little Kennedys filed into the room, shepherded by a cheerful couple in their early thirties. The three little girls ranged in age from four to thirteen and wore pristine white cotton dresses. The four little boys ranged from six to twelve and wore navy blazers. The candidate went down the line bestowing small fatherly benedictions of affection.

"Where have you been?"

"We've been to the zoo!"

Kennedy seized the youngest boy, hauled him over his head, and grasping his ankles, held him suspended behind his back.

"Where did he go?" said the candidate. "Has anybody seen David?"

David giggled and the other children looked bored by the familiar game.

"Here I am," said David, and his father acknowledged him with mock surprise.

"Where are we going today?" asked Robert Jr.

The candidate returned David to terra firma. "We're all going to a convention," he said.

"What's a convention?" said Michael.

"That's hard to explain. Especially for the candidates. But I want you all to be very good today." There was a general murmuring of assent as the children's mother lined them up preparatory to departure. Kennedy walked down the line straightening ties and replacing cowlicks. "Now be good. I'll have something for the one who's best."

The children started to march off. "And one more thing—" The heads turned attentively. "I'll *also* have something for the one who's *worst*."

With that admonition the children trouped out the door, and if one listened carefully, one could hear the strains of Richard Rodgers' "March of the Siamese Children."

The candidate retired to his bedroom to shave, dress, and glance over his acceptance speech one final time befor leaving for the convention. Meanwhile a thought occurred to me and I began to scribble fitfully on a yellow legal pad.

A quarter of an hour later Robert Kennedy, dressed in a suit of gray glen plaid and wearing the ubiquitous black tie that marked his mourning, returned to the living room and prepared to leave for the convention. As he paused a moment to glance at the clangorous TV set, I handed him a typewritten version of my scribbled thought and suggested it be incorporated in his labor speech for the following day.

[*15*]

His eyes gulped down the two pages and he returned it to me with an abstracted "That's good." And with that he turned and headed for the door.

Robert Kennedy's departure from his apartment was a marvelous sight to behold. He would simply say, "Let's go," and dart out the door. In the living room one of his aides would be feverishly packing schedules, speeches, and briefing papers into Kennedy's battered tan briefcase. In the bedroom another would be packing two clean shirts and assorted toiletries into a sleek black leather case. And with virtually no warning they would some-how contrive to catch up with the candidate before his car pulled away from the curb at 76th Street.

I gave the pages Kennedy had abstractedly approved to Angie Novello, who was starting to type the reading version of the labor speech, and indicated the place where they should be inserted. Then I left for the armory.

The convention armory was a sweltering, cavernous place. A perspiring, ill-tempered policeman directed me to the Kennedy box, a section of the balcony overlooking the convention floor—in fact, nearly overlooking it com-pletely. Already in the box were Peter Lawford, Eunice Kennedy Shriver, and a swirl of newsmen and camera-men. Lawford, his bronzed features expressing a mild distaste, was trying to answer a newsman's questions over the clamor of the crowd.

Meanwhile the convention floor was roiling. The dele-gates had been eagerly awaiting their candidate's arrival for over an hour—as audiences throughout the state would be doing for the next sixty days—patiently but with mounting anticipation.

Finally the convention chairman gaveled the hall to relative quiet, and using the mandatory form of introduction, shouted, "It is my great pleasure and privilege to present the next Senator from the State of New York, Robert F. Kennedy—"

And the armory went wild.

The band, sweltering in their garish uniforms just beneath us, struck up "Hello, Dolly." A string of policemen emerged from a door on the side of the hall and opened a perilously narrow aisle to the speaker's platform. Along this frail avenue, one by one, marched the Kennedy children. Then Ethel Kennedy, beaming radiantly, ran the gauntlet—an act not without its hazards for a woman five months with child. And then, when it seemed unlikely that the decibel level could rise any higher, the figure of the Attorney General emerged, and a great roar swept the armory.

Robert Kennedy delivered the speech with verve and conviction. Ethel looked on proudly, the picture of a Trojan woman, surrounded by her family. Little David wore a look of insupportable boredom. Kerry mugged shamefully at the TV camera.

And as I listened to the measured cadences, it became obvious to me that the candidate's most effective campaign speeches—like those of his brother—would be the ones he spoke, not the ones he read.

CHAPTER 3

>⋈<

The Reception

The acceptance speech ended the convention, and amidst slowly dying applause the Kennedys—husband, wife, and brood—followed the blue-coated line out of the arena.

The children were dispatched I know not where, and Mr. and Mrs. Robert Kennedy were driven the few crosstown blocks to the Sheraton-Atlantic Hotel, where a reception to end all receptions was being held for the delegates. Several large convention rooms were stocked with food and drink. Bartenders were at their stations. "Kennedy girls" in electric-blue dresses dotted the lobby. Placards and banners marked the walls. There was just one thing missing.

The delegates.

No one had bothered to invite them. The well-oiled Kennedy machine had triumphed again.

The result of this oversight was that aside from the handful of delegates who had heard of the affair by word of mouth, the place was deserted. The rest were now scattered to the four corners of New York, and this opportunity to enhance their feeling of good will was irremediably lost.

A reception line had been formed on the mezzanine, and Bob and Ethel Kennedy stood dutifully shaking the hands of those who, by the grace of God, were present.

Meanwhile the Kennedy people were trying desperately to retrieve some advantage from an impossible situation. They took off for the several department stores in the area, intent on rounding up all the unwary citizens they could corral for the reception. Said one astonished lady as she munched a canapé, "I was just coming out of Stern's and all of a sudden this girl grabs me. The next thing you know I'm shaking hands with Bobby!"

From the look of delight on the face of Ethel Kennedy and the placid look on the candidate's, one would never have suspected the dimensions of this gala fiasco. When he learned that the invitations had not been extended he grimaced and said, "I knew there was something wrong. Not enough people were wearing delegate badges and too many were carrying boxes marked Macy's."

The innocent bystanders, recently shanghaied from the stores and streets of New York, moved from the reception line into the rooms full of larder and levity. Though all the good Scotch and hors d'oeuvres would doubtless have done immeasurably more good had they been lavished on the delegates for whom they were intended, there is no denying that some faithful friends were made the day a thousand surprised New Yorkers were suddenly herded into the company of Bob and Ethel Kennedy and their largesse.

I was anxious to see the candidate after the reception that wasn't. Since his departure from the Carlyle that morning I had reread the pages he had so hastily approved, and I was having misgivings about whether they were perhaps too intemperate. So when Robert Kennedy was about to leave the Sheraton-Atlantic at 8:00 P.M. for a destination unknown to me, I outlined the problem to Ed Guthman.

"Just stay close to him when we leave," was the simple prescription.

It wasn't that easy.

To stay close to Robert Kennedy in a crowd, one needs the strength of a New York Giants lineman and the agility of the quarterback. I was separated from him at least six times as he proceeded, circled by a protective knot of patrolmen and detectives, down the stairs, through the lobby, and out to a waiting car that seemed to be surrounded by the entire population of Manhattan.

As the crowd swirled in on him, he strategically mounted the car roof to address them. (He and his aides caved in the roof of at least one car a day throughout the entire campaign. And one of the most frightening experiences you can imagine is to be *inside* the car as the candidate is battling for his footing on the roof.)

Seeing me flailing wildly in that ocean of people, Ed Guthman opened a way for me through the linked arms of the policemen to the Kennedy car. "Get in the back seat," he said. "Bob'll be in in a minute."

Finally the candidate hopped down from the car top, and a policeman opened the back door for him. Then things happened with startling suddenness. The policeman saw me, turned with alarm, and shouted, "Hey, there's somebody *in* here—" In a split second, police phalanx, candidate, and crowds wheeled away from the car, crossed the avenue to a waiting police car, and Robert Kennedy was carried off into the night.

I jumped out of the car and tried vainly to reach the Attorney General. It wasn't until I was standing rumpled and perplexed on Sixth Avenue that I put two and two together, as they say.

As Robert Kennedy was about to enter his car, a policeman saw a stranger—me—where none was supposed to be. The candidate was whisked away by secondary means. Perhaps there was some other explanation than the one that leaped to mind. At any rate, I never had the temerity to inquire.

I found a public telephone and called the dependable Miss Novello back at the Carlyle. "Where is the candidate heading now?" I asked.

"A private party at Le Pavillon."

I hesitated. Should I trouble him at a private party? Should I intrude on a family dinner regardless of the seeming urgency of my mission?

I made up my mind. My responsibility was clear. I hailed a cab.

"Le Pavillon, please."

CHAPTER 4

Le Pavillon

The cabbie had never heard of Le Pavillon.

I had heard of it, but never having dined there, I couldn't provide an address or even a street. I recalled a Kennedy credo: grace under pressure. "Look in your hack guide!" I stammered. He did so and said there was a Pavillon on Lenox and 125th Street, and another on Park and 57th Street. "It's probably the one on Park," I said.

At a large table near the entrance sat Robert and Ethel Kennedy, plus a dozen kith and kin. I approached the Attorney General, murmured an apology for my intrusion, and explained the reason for it, handing him a copy of the insert that had already been incorporated into his speech.

He read it through. "I don't know," he said. "It's strong, but it's effective . . . Why don't you join us?"

"Oh, I really wouldn't want to intrude," I said, wanting very much to intrude.

"Ethel, let Gerald get in over there."

"Well, hello again!" said Ethel Kennedy, making room for me beside her. "I want you to meet my sister-in-law, Pat Skakel, and this is Natalie Cushing, and Piedy Gimbel, and Lem Billings. You know Steve Smith, and this is his wife, Jean. This is Bob's sister, Eunice—" There were a few other names but I missed them. I said my hellos with laudable equanimity, I thought.

The candidate seemed quiet, abstracted, withdrawn from the animated group. Some of those at the table had the manner and look of high society and they seemed strangely out of place. There was a reality and natural-ness to the Kennedys that contrasted sharply with the carefully cultivated mien of the others. It occurred to me that Robert Kennedy had inherited some of these friends from his brother.

"They certainly gave Bobby a warm reception at the armory," said Eunice.

"Yes," said Ethel. "I think it's because they know he *cares*."

It was at that moment that historian Arthur Schlesinger, Jr., and Washington columnist Rowland Evans—close friends of the Kennedys—entered the restaurant and were greeted warmly by the table at large. There began a great shifting about to permit them to join us, but the table was already hopelessly overcrowded.

"There doesn't seem to be any room for us," said Schlesinger with mock bitterness. "We fly all the way up from Washington for this gala occasion and that's the reception we get."

"Well," said Evans, turning on his heel, "we can just make the ten o'clock shuttle."

"Don't be silly, Rolly," piped Ethel Kennedy. "There's room here between Jean and me."

Evans moved in on Ethel's left, and Schlesinger and the Steve Smiths moved to an adjoining table.

Suddenly Ethel seized my arm and pointed down the table to a ruddy, smiling young man who had joined the group a few minutes before.

"Do you know who that is?" said Ethel.

"No," I admitted.

"That's Tom Corcoran—one of the greatest skiers in America."

"I think we'd better be going," said the candidate.

"Gerald," said Ethel, "what do you think about a tie clasp in the shape of the State of New York, with the word *Kennedy* on Long Island?"

"Good idea," I said.

"Teddy had these wonderful tie clasps in the shape of the State of Massachusetts."

"Of course," I observed, "the shape of New York isn't quite as regular as that of Massachusetts."

"That's true," said Ethel.

"And putting the name on Long Island would make it awfully small, as well as identifying Bob with New York *City* rather than with the whole state."

"That's true," said Ethel. "But you do like the idea, don't you?"

"I think we'd better be going," said the candidate for the second time, as mildly as he had the first. This time the suggestion took. Ethel rose and started to edge her way out from behind the table.

"Bobby has to be at the Fulton Fish Market at 4:30 A.M.," explained Ethel.

"Wouldn't you think," I said, "that for Robert Kennedy they would deliver?"

CHAPTER 5

The Endorsement

Before he left Le Pavillon, bound for three hours' sleep and a date with some halibut, Robert Kennedy had asked if I could be at his apartment at nine the following morning—practically midday for him. I said I could.

I arrived at the Carlyle at ten minutes of nine, was admitted by Angie Novello, and walked into a living room occupied by a battalion of children. There were children eating breakfast, children watching television, children scaling paper airplanes. And imperturbably, through it all, there was Ethel Kennedy poring over the *New York Times*.

"Good morning," she said brightly. "I don't suppose you can work in here."

"Oh, that's all right," I said, opening my attaché case and dodging a paper airplane coming in at three o'clock. "Well, perhaps I'll find an empty bedroom."

But finding an empty bedroom was easier said than done. The suite had three of them, two baths, a living room, and a kitchenette, but there seemed to be enough little Kennedys to go around. I decided my best bet was the bedroom in which Kerry, the Kennedys' youngest daughter, was scaling her paper airplanes. Since I have a son of four and Kerry's behavior and speech resembled his, I knew instinctively she must be four years old.

"How old are you?" I said.

"I'm four years old," said Kerry Kennedy.

I smiled confidently. "I have a little boy your age," I said.

"Can he make a paper airplane?" she said.

I winced.

At about ten o'clock Bob Kennedy returned from his campaign visit to the Fulton Fish Market, looking like a man who has had three hours' sleep and then visited the Fulton Fish Market. He now had a full hour to kill before it was time to leave for the Hotel Commodore to convince the delegates of the strongest union in the state that they should endorse him.

The candidate turned to Ed Guthman. "Do you think Ethel should come? Would she be helpful?"

"I would think so," said Guthman, who was busy stuffing papers into Kennedy's crowded briefcase.

Kennedy strode from the room. He returned a few moments later. "She says she'll come, but we'll have to wait a few minutes while she does something with her hair."

As we waited Kennedy picked up a copy of a newspaper that lay on a table in the hall. It was opened to a column whose headline bore his name: WHY DOES BOBBY DUCK CIVIL RIGHTS? it asked. The burden of the columnist's message was that Kennedy had been in the forefront of the fight for civil rights during the past four years, yet he had not as yet mentioned it in the campaign, and this was interpreted as a craven fear of white backlash.

Kennedy threw down the newspaper with a ponderous sigh.

Ten minutes later the Kennedys were in a Pontiac Bonneville, heading downtown toward the Commodore Hotel. They were running late and his driver wheeled the car onto Madison Avenue, then braked sharply to avoid hitting a bus. Kennedy put his arm protectively around his wife. "Take it easy. I'd rather be late."

The candidate had planned to make a brief stop on the way to the Commodore to visit some influential party leaders. "There won't be time," he now said. "We should let them know I can't see them. We need a phone in this car."

"We'll get a phone in the next one," said Guthman, which meant, I suppose, as soon as the candidate caved in the roof of this one.

As Bob Kennedy reached the periphery of the Commodore ballroom, a buzz of excitement radiated across the room. The convention proceedings suddenly came to a standstill as every man in the hall turned his head, rose from his chair, and broke into sustained applause as the candidate and his wife wove their way around the room to the platform.

Just before the crowd engulfed him, Robert Kennedy turned to me and said, "I hope I do justice to your speech." And then he was gone.

He delivered the speech and yet he didn't. The points

were all there, yet they came out stronger, more cogent, more electric. For the candidate did not read the speech —he translated it into extemporaneous terms.

The eight hundred union delegates in the hall interrupted him repeatedly with lengthy applause, frequently standing *en masse* to emphasize their enthusiasm.

At the close of the speech Mr. and Mrs. Robert Kennedy wound their way back to the entrance door, their faces ablaze with the lights of movie cameramen. And over the tumult of the crowd, a loudspeaker carried a voice intoning, "This convention endorses Robert F. Kennedy by acclamation!"

There was the quality of conquest in this moment— the quality of the matador leaving the arena with the ears of *el toro*.

From the Commodore we drove to the Overseas Press Club, where a cocktail party was being tendered in the candidate's behalf to the political writers of New York's newspapers and magazines. This time the invitations reached the guests.

Robert Kennedy moved easily among them. An intense-looking young woman named Judy Michaelson introduced herself. "I'm with the *New York Post*," she said, "and this is my first campaign."

"Mine too," said Kennedy. "We better stay close together."

Debs Myers, who had arranged the affair, introduced me to a reporter named Nick Timmisch. Timmisch had an ironic, faintly haughty manner that made me think of *Time* magazine.

"Nick is with *Time* magazine," said Debs.

As Kennedy roamed the room, stopping to talk to little knots of people, I chatted with Timmisch. As I responded to his questions, I tried to picture each of my answers quoted out of context. It was an uncomfortable few minutes.

Half an hour later, as we emerged from the Overseas Press Club, the candidate was suddenly surrounded by a group of nuns. They fluttered about him, shaking his hand, taking his arm, and soliciting his autograph.

As he finally disengaged himself and entered his waiting car, he said, "It's one of the great unsolved mysteries. All the nuns love me and none of the priests do."

The Bonneville fought its way through the five o'clock crosstown traffic. We were already late for the next stop on our schedule. Kennedy's driver, a New York detective named Jim King, was doing his best, adroitly cutting off cursing taxi drivers.

"You're losing me the cabbie vote," said Kennedy.

"Cabbies hate everybody," said King. "I don't think they vote for *anyone.*"

The car moved forward another few yards and then came to a standstill again, hopelessly trapped in traffic.

"Who says I don't know anything about the problems of New York?" said Kennedy dryly. "How far are we from where we're going?"

"About three blocks," said King.

"Well, in that case—" said Kennedy, then flung open the door, and headed for the sidewalk with his aides in hot pursuit.

As Kennedy strode purposefully down 51st Street, I observed one of the truly satisfying phenomena of the campaign. It was the sudden transformation of the face of a New Yorker from preoccupation to delight when he sees Robert Kennedy bearing down on him.

The change bears description, perhaps in a medical journal. First there is incredulity, which turns rapidly to certainty, followed by excitement and a desire to communicate one's finding to a companion. The favored exclamation is, "It's Bobby!"

Needless to say, the candidate's progress as a pedestrian was not perceptibly faster than it had been as a traffic-jammed motorist. But now at least the delays had their virtues—and their votes.

As we reached the hotel that was our destination, Ed Guthman said, "I've just devised a winning strategy for you, Bob."

Kennedy questioned him with a look.

"All you have to do is walk up and down the streets of New York. Everyone who sees you tells fifty friends. In no time that adds up to a majority."

"It will," said Kennedy, "if they vote for me."

And that was the great imponderable of the campaign. Would the people who turned out to see him in such great numbers, who shouted his name and crushed his hand, who mobbed and mauled him—would they vote for him?

CHAPTER 6

ⱶ✕ᛏ

The Trip Upstate

The pale blue Bonneville carrying Robert Kennedy and three of his aides turned into the East River Drive at 96th Street and headed north. Its destination: LaGuardia Airport and the candidate's first upstate swing. His stops would include the city of Syracuse and two resorts in the Catskill Mountains—Grossinger's and the Concord—which would be crowded over this Labor Day weekend.

The car wheeled onto the private landing strip at LaGuardia's Marine Terminal, where a group of newsmen stood beside a twin-engined plane that shone white in the early-morning sunlight. On its nose, lettered in elegant script, was the name *Caroline*.

In 1960 the *Caroline* had carried John Kennedy and his staff—Ted Sorensen, Pierre Salinger, Robert Kennedy—across America on another journey. Now Robert Kennedy would sit in the candidate's seat, and though traveling a more abridged geography, he would face an equally demanding schedule, with the outcome equally in doubt.

The candidate stood by the *Caroline's* ramp as a motion picture cameraman recorded the event. With luck, the film and Kennedy's desultory remarks would be carried on the evening's eleven o'clock news broadcasts.

The newsmen from the New York papers waited dutifully. Among them, Nick Timmisch of *Time* stood out. The others wore conservative business suits. Timmisch wore sports clothes.

"You look comfortable," I said.

"I heard Grossinger's was on the schedule," said Timmisch.

It was an interesting group. R. W. "Johnny" Apple of the *Times*, cherubic and bright; Terry Smith of the *Tribune*, wry offspring of sports columnist Red Smith; Judy Michaelson, the intense, unsmiling girl from the *Post* on her first campaign; Les Whitten of the *Journal*, full of literary allusions; and Frank Lynn of the *Telegram*, interested and outgoing.

Curiously enough, all appeared to be in their thirties, almost as though the editors of New York's dailies had thought that people of that age would be best equipped to report the political launching of the thirty-eight-year-old candidate.

The *Caroline* is a most comfortable plane. Six pairs of seats face one another across desks with built-in accommodations for glasses. The glasses, containing your liquid preferences, are provided by an attractive, un-uniformed stewardess named Jan. Close at hand are all the day's papers and all the week's magazines.

The candidate's seat is set somewhat apart, and he could usually be found spooning soup, sipping beer, studying a speech, or reading a fact sheet dealing with the next stop on his crowded itinerary.

The fact sheets were tributes to research and concision.

On one tightly typed page, here is what it told the candidate about the town of Catskill.

Population: 6000

Economy: Declared a depressed area. Help needed to improve resort activities, attract vacationers.

Dairy farmers going out of business due to high costs and inadequate price support.

Ethnic: Italian 21%
German 27%
Irish 8%
Negro: 75 families, employed in brickyards and distilleries.
Italians: in knit goods factories.

Background: Catskill in valley of Catskill Creek. Originally known as Catskill Landing. Settled in 1662 by Dutch. At west end is Rip Van Winkle Bridge.

Painter Thomas Cole is from Catskill, founded Academy of Design.

Politics: Board of Supervisors is 11-3 Republican.

Issues:
Roads and Highways: Road needed to short-cut to Roscoe.
River Purification: Sewage disposal plant needed.
Medicare: Sentiment is for it. High over-65 population here.
Education: Big drop-out problem. School taxes rising sharply.
Conservation: Greeks (*sic*) and rivers must be dammed up.

[*34*]

The *Caroline* made a perfect landing at Syracuse's Hancock Airport, and the reporters and candidate joined in a spontaneous outburst of applause. This expression of gratitude for the pilot's skill occurred at every landing.

"We started the practice during Jack's campaign back in 'sixty," said one of the newsmen.

If there was any doubt that Robert Kennedy's appeal did not extend north of the Bronx, it was quickly laid to rest as he climbed down the ramp from the *Caroline* at Hancock Airport. A crowd of eight hundred greeted him where forty had welcomed his opponent the day before. The crowd lined the fence that rimmed the field. Kennedy walked to the far end of the fence and began walking slowly but steadily along its length, both hands extended into the crowd. Around and behind him trailed policemen, aides, photographers, and small children who had hopped the fence for a closer look. A swarm of teenage girls, each with a red *S* emblazoned on her sweater, sang adenoidally :

> *We love you, Bobby,*
> *Oh, yes, we do-oo,*
> *And to you, Bobby,*
> *We will be true-oo.*
> *When you're not near us*
> *We're blue.*
> *Oh, Bobby, we love you.*

Kennedy continued along the wire fence as the four-deep throng behind it plucked at his hands and the cuffs of his meticulously tailored gray worsted suit. Occasionally he would stop to take a proffered pen and scribble his all but illegible initials. A girl gasped as he shook her outstretched hand, looked joyfully at the hand, and then began to bounce on her tiptoes. A man holding a toddler on his shoulders crushed the candidate's hand in a show of sincerity and affection.

As the candidate moved down the line, it seemed, incredibly, to be extending itself further and further along the airport fence, like some self-propagating dragon's tail that continues to grow as you cut it off. Suddenly the candidate realized what was happening. "As soon as they shake my hand, they run to the end of the line," he said to no one in particular, and left the fence with another fifty feet of voters still untouched.

The first stop in our motorcade through Syracuse was at the dedication ceremonies for the newly opened John F. Kennedy Park. The Mayor took command of the microphone to give a lengthy speech extolling the accomplishments of his city administration. On and on rolled the self-serving rhetoric, every line further abusing the tight Kennedy schedule. The candidate stood waiting for this display of oratorical vanity to end. There was no sign of the impatience and irritation he must have been feeling.

Seeing Robert Kennedy on a platform, standing beside a clutch of Democratic politicians, one recalled the comment of Murray Kempton in his maiden column in the *New York World-Telegram* the previous week. When you saw Bob Kennedy among politicians, observed Kempton, you saw that here was a *thoroughbred*.

When the candidate was finally introduced, his remarks were brief, but not abrupt. He closed by invoking the wisdom of George Bernard Shaw and stepped down. The crowd crushed in on him, and his aides knifed through them toward their convertible.

I mounted the press bus and took the seat beside a secretary, Carol Ash. Carol had a fresh-scrubbed innocence that led one newsman to observe, "All the Kennedy secretaries have the look of the nunnery. I think it's to help the press keep their mind on the campaign."

Carol Ash carried an oversized handbag of multicolored burlap—in other words, a carpetbag. As the bus got under way, Nick Timmisch slid into a seat opposite us, leaned across the aisle, and whispered to me conspiratorially, "Who's the girl? Reporter from *Women's Wear Daily?*"

"No, her name's Ash. Secretary for the candidate." Timmisch scribbled a note.

"How do you do, Miss Ash? That's a very handsome carpetbag."

"Now wait a minute," said Carol. "I just carry this because it's roomy and it's a good thing to have when you're far from home."

"Far from home, eh?" said Timmisch, smiling delightedly. "Better and better," and he made another note.

At the front of the bus a handful of press photographers stood before the panoramic windows and snapped the candidate as the boys and girls from Syracuse ran up to his slowly moving open car to shake his hand. There was an aspect of danger when children on bicycles rode alongside the car and reached out a hand to touch the candidate. They could have fallen from their bikes in the path of the bus. But the photographers encouraged the practice since the scene made a most effective photo.

"Come on," shouted a photographer as a ten-year-old pedaled frantically, trying to overtake the car. "Come on, you can make it—"

Our next stop was the Syracuse State Fair. Fair officials had predicted a turnout of thirty thousand on this their opening day. But that was before news of Robert Kennedy's presence had appeared in the Syracuse papers. The conservative *New York Times* estimated the turnout at a conservative fifty thousand. And this in a heavily Republican area. Kennedy's first upstate swing was taking on the characteristics of a wild triumphal march.

The candidate had battled his way to the grandstand that must have quivered often to the beat of John Philip Sousa. The crowd swarmed about the bandstand, packed tightly together.

Finally the obligatory words went bellowing across the fairgrounds—"The next Senator from the State of New York, Robert Francis Kennedy."

The candidate stepped to the microphone and surveyed the crowd crushing in on the platform. Above the cheers and applause he heard the whimper of a child coming from the base of the bandstand. Kennedy reached down and plucked out of the crowd a six-year-old girl who was on the edge of panic from the stifling crush that had threatened her. Kennedy carried her to the rear of the platform while the audience waited impatiently, uncertain of what was delaying the long-awaited speech.

"Now you stay here with Mr. Guthman. There's

nothing to cry about. I haven't started to speak yet—"
That brought a giggle and the candidate smiled and returned to the microphone.

"There has been a great deal of talk," he began, "about why I came to New York. I'd like to explain that, so when any of *you* are asked about it, you'll know what to say.

"I was born in New York—I grew up here—went to school here—held my first job here. I always felt a great fondness for the State of New York. Then I went away to college, went away to service, and went away to work in Washington. But I always felt that I'd like to repay New York for those wonderful years."

The audience applauded his sincerity, not knowing what was coming. I didn't know what was coming myself, but I was beginning to suspect.

"Then a few months ago," said the candidate in the same guileless tone, "I was having breakfast with my wife. And I was reading in the papers that California had replaced New York as the number one state in population—"

Utter silence. Kennedy waited, and his instinct was rewarded. The laughter started in the back, and as comprehension grew, it swept the crowd.

"So I turned to my wife and I said, 'What can we *do?*'" Full-bodied laughter, louder than before. "So I moved to New York, and in just one day I increased the population by ten and a half." More laughter. "And I challenge any other Senatorial candidate to make that statement." Laughter turning to applause.

But the candidate had one more turn of the screw. His

index finger prodded the air. "My opponent has just sixty days to match that record."

From Syracuse we invaded the "borscht belt." We took a small two-engine craft to Liberty Airport—the same type of plane in which Ted Kennedy had crashed several months before. Liberty Airport, it seemed, was not equipped to accommodate the *Caroline,* yet the local politicos of Liberty had arranged an airport rally and could not be disappointed.

So while most of the press contingent took the *Caroline* to another nearby airport, the candidate, his aides, and three chosen reporters rattled into Liberty in relative discomfort.

Terry Smith of the *Tribune* and Johnny Apple of the *Times* were tapping out the Syracuse story on Olivetti typewriters balanced on their laps, no mean feat in the dipping, vibrating craft.

"What did he say at the Fair?" said Smith. "I was too far back in the crush."

Apple began to relate the marathon joke about Kennedy's prolificness as the little plane circled the field preparing to land. The candidate pressed his forehead to the window and stared down at the crowd of about three thousand that dotted the field.

"Look down there!" he said eagerly. "I think I see two people who are over twenty-one—"

The airport rally was spirited. The tall, hatchet-faced man who introduced Bob Kennedy must have been conscripted from a local hotel floor show. The tone of his introduction was that of a master of ceremonies bringing on the night's headliner.

"And now, ladies and gentlemen," he said, "it is my great pleasure to present to you one of the great people of our time, and here he is to speak to you tonight, so let's hear it for the next Senator from the State of New York, John F.—" The crowd gasped and the master of ceremonies turned ashen. "I mean Robert F. Kennedy."

Darkness was coming on rapidly as our motorcade took us the few miles to Grossinger's. Jenny Grossinger, the legendary mistress of this sour-cream mecca, received the candidate warmly and excitedly. She had arranged, she said, "a small party" in her cottage on the grounds. "I've invited just a privileged few," she bubbled. The privileged few appeared to number fifty percent of her Labor Day guest list.

Jenny Grossinger kept darting about the room, followed by a little man with sharp features and black button eyes. "Have a glass of No-Cal Cola," she said, extending a glass to Kennedy. "It's good."

The little man now pigeonholed me. "Are you one of Kennedy's aides?"

"That's right."

"You write his speeches?"

"Some of them."

"I have some valuable facts for his speeches," he said, shuffling some papers and blinking his eyes very rapidly.

"You don't say?"

"For instance, did you know that the town of Liberty was established by a man from Massachusetts?"

"No, I didn't," I said. "That would be very helpful to the Attorney General. I'd welcome anything of that sort you could—"

"Wait a minute! Wait a minute!" he said. "You don't think I'm just *giving* this stuff away. I'm not a boy just out of Princeton," he added.

"Oh, I didn't know."

"Of course not," said button-eyes. "Now what do you say?"

"Perhaps you'd better speak to Bill vandenHeuvel," I said, leaping behind the safety of another name. "He's Mr. Kennedy's *chief* speechwriter."

The candidate was leaving and I followed him out through the host of well-wishers—women in tinseled gowns, with hair piled high as a honeycomb; men in sleek, tight-fitting tuxedos and with dull Miami tans. Kennedy bored his way out of the cottage, across the darkened grounds, and into the main dining room, where dinner was in progress. A line of handsomely coiffed women materialized in his path.

"Isn't he beautiful?"

"He's a doll!"

"He's like a little boy."

"I touched him!"

This last was from a middle-aged manufacturer with a faceful of broken commandments.

Jenny Grossinger and the candidate mounted a table at the back of the dining room. The diners turned in their seats and many of them converged on the table.

"The man who stands beside me is *loved*," said Jenny Grossinger with feeling. "We love him as we loved his brother and as we love his whole family. I give you—Bob Kennedy."

The squeals and applause finally died, and Kennedy said, "If the Kennedys are a close-knit family and if we are very fierce in our loyalty to one another, we have the Jewish people to thank. I remember when my father was out in Hollywood in the movie business, he spent a good deal of time with the Warner brothers and with Sam Goldwyn. And he saw how they raised their children to be loyal and to be respectful of their parents. And he decided to bring his own children up that way."

The diners applauded lustily as their soup cooled.

Now the candidate turned to a more familiar target. "Senator Keating offered to send me a road map. Well, I don't need a road map to know how I feel about Barry Goldwater. I'm against Barry Goldwater." The invocation of the dreaded name brought cheers. It always did.

"Barry Goldwater wants to give control of nuclear weapons to commanders in the field. Now that's my idea of high adventure. General Eisenhower says that he could *live* with a Goldwater Administration. Well, I suppose he'd have as good a chance as anyone else."

The diners laughed heartily. The soup was now inedible, but no one seemed to care. Bob Kennedy was the best thing on the menu and they were enjoying him.

"So I come here to Grossinger's and I ask for your help. And I think what should guide us"—Smith of the *Trib* and Apple of the *Times* winced at the familiar closing line—"is what George Bernard Shaw said—" Whitten of the *Journal* began to recite soundlessly the Shavian epigram along with the candidate. "Some people

[*43*]

see things as they are and say *why*. I dream things that never were and say *why not?*"

Our next stop was the Concord Hotel, where events paralleled those at Grossinger's in most respects, except that the women's hair was piled, on the average, two centimeters higher.

"The Catskills," Kennedy observed to the diners in the Concord's cavernous dining room, "were immortalized by Washington Irving. He wrote of a man who fell asleep and awoke in another era. The only other area that can boast such a man is Phoenix, Arizona."

The final stop of the long day's journey was the Roosevelt Raceway. The candidate was scheduled to present a cup to the winner of the fourth race. As the motorcade rolled along the main street of Ellenville on the way to the raceway, Kennedy told his driver to stop, and jumped from the car.

It seemed a curious thing to do. The streets were all but deserted. Yet with the press following behind him, Bob Kennedy started walking briskly down the sidewalk. Within five minutes there were several hundred people converged on the candidate, all traffic had stopped, cars were abandoned, candy stores, restaurants, and bowling alleys disgorged hordes of people as word flashed along.

"It's Bobby Kennedy!"

"Where?"

"Right here!"

"Where here?"

"Here—on the street!"

Having hopelessly tangled the Main Street traffic and made it a most eventful evening for the citizens of Ellenville, Robert Kennedy returned to his car wearing a look of quiet satisfaction.

As we entered the large oval area beneath the grandstand at the Roosevelt Raceway, a drunk shook his fist at the candidate and shouted a string of obscenities as he passed. But as Kennedy came out into the grandstand he was greeted by applause that rippled outward as word raced along of his arrival. The stands with their steep stairwells and narrow aisles immobilized both candidate and spectators—they could not converge on him, nor was there any facility available that would enable him to address them.

Kennedy made the best of a less than ideal political arena. He stood on a seat in the lowest tier of the grandstand section. Bathed in the lights of news cameramen and readily seen by the thousands above him, Kennedy received their applause.

The fourth race was about to begin and the stadium lights went dim. Kennedy settled down in an anonymous seat to watch it. There was little wagered on the winning horse, or on any of the others in the fourth race. With Kennedy in the grandstand, few people felt inclined to leave their seats to place a bet.

When the race had ended, a line of policemen opened a path for the candidate as he proceeded to the winner's circle to present the award. One massive enforcer of the law was laboring mightily and cursing softly as he held back the crushing crowds. A Keating man in the making, I thought. Suddenly he tore the cover from his book of summonses and thrust it at me. "Can you get me Bobby's signature?" he said.

I put the square of pasteboard in my pocket. "I'll do my best," I said.

In a few minutes Kennedy was again striding back toward the cars of our motorcade, which were strung along the road by the entrance to the raceway. It was nearly midnight and it had been a long day. The cars set out for the airport, where the *Caroline* waited to return us to New York.

As we drove along a lonely stretch of country road, Kennedy noticed three little girls, age nine or ten, pointing excitedly after the candidate's car. "Hold it," he said. Jim King braked the car smoothly and the seven cars following also drew to a halt.

The heads of exhausted reporters projected from car windows along the line. There could be no supportable reason for stopping out here in the dead of night.

Kennedy jumped from the car, trotted back along the darkened road to where the little girls were, and bent over to talk to them. The children stared at him with unbelieving eyes. He rumpled their hair, then went back to the car as the girls clapped their hands over their mouths and bounced up and down in excitement.

"Okay, let's go," said the candidate, and the motorcade continued on toward the airport.

CHAPTER 7

The Cove

Heading back to LaGuardia Airport after his day-long swing upstate, the candidate leaned across the aisle that separated us. "Can you come out to Glen Cove for lunch tomorrow?"

I said I could.

I arrived at the big white house—a twenty-five-room Dutch colonial he had leased from a successful fashion designer—and found Kennedy's solemn aide, Dean Markham, in tennis clothes.

"Bob's off somewhere watching his kids in a swimming meet," said Markham, and ambled off.

I entered the living room and noticed prominently positioned on the window sill a framed photograph of the candidate's son David on the White House grounds. The picture bore the inscription: "A future President inspects his property." It was signed "John F. Kennedy."

On another wall was a page from a yellow legal pad, framed in black. The black-bordered card inset beneath it carried these words in a graceful feminine script:

*Notes made by President Kennedy at his last
Cabinet Meeting, October 29, 1963.
For Robert Kennedy.*

Jackie

The lined page was covered with words and numbers. There were the words "soy beans" and "baby beans" and "poverty"—the last repeated many times. There was the number "2½ million" repeated again and again. There was the word "satellites." And there—dominating the center of the page—was a freehand sketch of a sailboat, tall and cool on a quiet lake.

"Hello there," said a voice behind me. I turned and found Ethel Kennedy.

"Hello," I said, and noticed again the pale-pink lipstick, the bubbling speech, the look of wonderment.

"How did you do in Brooklyn?" I said.

The day before Ethel Kennedy had climbed a ladder to the top of a sound truck in downtown Brooklyn, mounted an insecure wooden platform, and officially opened her husband's borough headquarters.

"All right, I suppose," said Ethel. "I told them Bobby was upstate and I had come to Brooklyn to be among friends."

"Good thinking," I said.

"Listen," said Ethel Kennedy, "you must know a lot of people in show business. Could you get me someone to perform at our Drop-out Affair?"

"Your what?"

"Our Drop-out Affair."

"What's that? A teen-age love song?"

"No," said Ethel patiently. "When we were in Washington, Bobby set up this group to keep youngsters from dropping out of school. Next week they're putting on a show to raise money. Sammy Davis has promised to entertain. Now what we need is someone famous to come out and introduce him."

"And what star wouldn't give his eyeteeth to do *that?*" I said dryly.

"Well, he could entertain too, if he wanted to."

"How about Robert Morse?" I said.

"Wonderful!" said Ethel. "I loved him in *How to Succeed.*"

"I'll call him," I said.

"I'll speak to Pat Lawford, too," said Ethel. "She's our *other* contact with the entertainment world."

A housekeeper entered and told Mrs. Kennedy she was wanted on the phone.

"See you later," she said and was gone.

A few minutes later Robert Kennedy entered the house, flanked by sons David and Bobby, and daughter Kathleen. The candidate wore a pullover sweater, khaki shorts, and sneakers. His face was taking on a deep tan from exposure to sun and wind in the open cars of countless motorcades. His posture made him seem shorter than his five feet ten inches.

"Let's go out by the pool," he said, and we strolled to the padded wrought-iron furniture that bordered the large swimming pool behind the house.

He took a chair facing the sun and squinted up into it. Here was the Kennedy magnetism—the cleft chin, the blue eyes, the clump of sandy hair. Here was the weathered face that set women to squealing and bouncing and jiggling on their tiptoes as he passed.

"I hear you've written a campaign song," he said.

I passed him a sheet of paper with parodied lyrics to the song "Hello, Dolly." He scanned it and promptly turned toward the lawn where David, Bobby, and Kathleen were struggling for possession of a football.

"Time out!" called the candidate. "Come here a minute." The children trotted over and he extended the sheet to them. "Let's hear you sing this. It's to the tune of 'Hello, Dolly.' "

The three took the paper and trudged soberly back several paces, like a football squad going back to their huddle. They pored over the lyrics and then returned to us at poolside.

"Ready for your audition?" said Robert Kennedy.

They nodded and launched into song.

Hello, Bobby,
Well, hello, Bobby,
It's so nice to have you back where you belong.
The Empire State, Bobby,
Rates you great, Bobby,
From the Brooklyn Bridge to Buffalo you're going strong.

The candidate flashed an appreciative smile—whether in appreciation of his children's vocal gifts or my lyrical ones, I am not sure—but I could guess.

In Washington, Bobby,
When you've won, Bobby,
You will get New York to really move again,
So no retreat, fellas,
Get him a Senate seat, fellas,
Bobby will never go away again.

Robert Kennedy, looking like a proud parent, applauded. David, Bobby Jr., and Kathleen, looking like frustrated football players, dropped the paper and ran.

"That last line," said the candidate, "about my never going away again—"

"It doesn't say positively," I said.

"Speak to Pat Lawford about this. You can call her at the Cape. She's working on a campaign song with Mitch Miller."

Poor Senator Keating, I thought. Not enough to face the combined recriminations of Kennedy, Wagner, Harriman, and Franklin Roosevelt, Jr. Now Mitch Miller!

The candidate rose from his chair and joined his abbreviated brood on the lawn. His lithe body wheeled among them, trying to elude their touch.

I climbed back up the flagstone steps leading to the house, found a phone in the den, and dialed Pat Lawford on Cape Cod.

"Hello?" said a soprano voice.

"Mrs. Lawford?"

"Yes."

"Bob asked me to call you about a campaign song—"

"Oh yes, a campaign song. We already have one. It's to the tune of 'There's Gonna Be a Great Day.' "

"That sounds great," I said.

"It's very bouncy. Mitch Miller is going to record it so we can play it from all the sound trucks."

"Good thinking."

"What's *your* campaign song like?"

"It's to the tune of 'Hello, Dolly,' " I said.

"Read me the lyrics," said Mrs. Lawford. "Slowly. I want to copy them down." I did and she did.

"You'll have to call the White House," said Pat Lawford.

"Oh?"

"To see if the President would mind Bob using it. It's his theme song, too, you know. Carol Channing sang it to him at Atlantic City."

"I see."

"So first you'll have to clear it with Mr. Johnson. Then will come the hard part."

"What's that?" I said.

"You'll have to clear it with David Merrick."

CHAPTER 8

The Visit

The mimeographed schedule for the day began with this item: 10:15 A.M. Visit former Kennedy residence— 5040 Independence Avenue, Riverdale, Bronx—Mr. and Mrs. Sills.

As the campaign swept along, concern was growing because the carpetbagger issue would not go away. Kennedy had tried to bypass it with humor. He had concentrated on what he viewed to be the real issues. He had assumed the voters would make their judgment on the candidates' qualifications, not the candidates' addresses.

"I lived in New York for many years," he said. "But if this election is to be decided on the basis of who's lived here the longest, perhaps we should just elect the oldest man in the state."

But the issue had not gone away. The polls revealed the greatest single source of antipathy to Robert Kennedy was the view that he was a brash young interloper from out of the state. Virtually no one the canvassers questioned appeared to know that for most of the first twenty years of his life, Robert Kennedy's home was in New

York State. Hence the first stop on the day's schedule was his old home in Riverdale, New York. The purpose —to focus attention on his early residence in the state.

When Robert Kennedy entered the elevator on the eleventh floor of the Carlyle that morning, he found a three-year-old boy in short red pants, a knitted white sweater, and a circle of chocolate candy around his mouth. It was John F. Kennedy, Jr. He had just descended from his mother's apartment on the fourteenth floor and was waiting, under the watchful eye of the elevator man, to join the campaign train.

"Don't call him John-John," Kennedy cautioned. Then he bent to his nephew. "Good morning, John."

The boy clutched a large red stuffed dolphin.

"What's his name?" asked the candidate.

"This is Flipper," said John with a lisp.

"Oh yes," said his uncle. "There's a movie about him. Have you seen the movie?" John soberly shook his head. "Well, we'll have to take you to see *Flipper* if it's still playing."

"It's been held under another week," I said. The candidate groaned.

We drove north along Henry Hudson Parkway, Kennedy in the front seat with John and Flipper.

Soon we left the highway and drove through the empty streets of the Riverdale section of the Bronx, and finally came to a stop before a church on Riverdale Avenue. The candidate turned to his nephew. "Your father was confirmed here," he said simply. Then the two entered the church.

A few minutes later they returned to the car and we drove on.

"Did you move to Riverdale from Brookline?" I asked.

"Yes, Brookline," said the candidate, and smiled wanly. "Averell got that a little mixed up the other night," he said, referring to former Governor Harriman, who had been campaigning with him. "He introduced me at a Brooklyn rally as a local boy. I explained to him afterward that it was Brook*line*. In Massachusetts."

The car rolled on through the quiet streets.

"It's funny when you think of it," said Kennedy. "Did you know they called my brother John a carpetbagger when he ran in Massachusetts? They said he should be running in New York." He squinted out the window at the quiet houses and the streets lined with their carpet of autumn leaves.

Bob Kennedy had started in Riverdale's public schools but before long he had been shifted through a couple of private schools. Then the family moved to Bronxville, New York, and he was enrolled in the Bronxville public schools.

"Didn't you have a magazine route in Riverdale?" said King.

"No, that was in Bronxville." The candidate smiled wryly. "I was very enterprising."

Ethel had told me about the magazine route. Bobby's brother Joe had presented him with a pig that he had promptly named "Porky." While his father was busy conquering Wall Street, Bob Kennedy had tried his own hand at commercial conquest—as a salesman for the *Ladies' Home Journal* and the *Saturday Evening Post.*

"When he started," Ethel had said, "there was Bobby delivering magazines from his bicycle with Porky following along behind. The next thing the neighbors saw was Bobby and his magazines in the back seat of the family Rolls-Royce and the chauffeur driving him around to make sales.

"Finally," concluded Ethel, "the chauffeur was all by himself with the magazines, and you could barely get into Bobby's room, there were so many unsold magazines around!"

The car pulled into the circular driveway of a two-story white stucco house on Independence Avenue.

"Hold it a minute," snapped the candidate as he saw a busload of reporters and cameramen camped at the front door. Kennedy looked down at John playing with Flipper. "Dean, get out and tell them there's to be no pictures. Absolutely no pictures."

Markham jumped out of the car and trotted over to the knot of cameramen. A few minutes later he was back. "All right, Bob, they've agreed."

We drove up to the house and the candidate disembarked with John Kennedy, Jr., in tow. A sizable crowd of neighborhood children was clustered along the sidewalk and followed the candidate as he strolled up the driveway. Everywhere Kennedy went, a score of children seemed to follow in his wake. In fact, the metaphor that became a journalistic cliché virtually overnight was "Robert Kennedy, the modern-day Pied Piper."

The two Kennedys knocked and were admitted to the

house by Mr. and Mrs. Philip Sills, the present owners. Their coolness, under the circumstances, led me to suspect they must be Republicans. (Mr. Sills, a manufacturing executive, later told reporters that he was a Democrat but he had not yet decided whether to vote for Kennedy or Keating.)

The newsmen waited outside while Robert and John were shown through the house and then out the kitchen door onto the spacious back lawn where more than thirty years before young Kennedys had romped and leaped.

After a few minutes Bob Kennedy climbed the back porch, holding John by the ankles, behind his back. "John—where are you? Has anyone seen John?"

Mrs. Sills had a large urn of coffee, a trayful of coffee cups, and some Danish pastry. "Will you have some coffee, Mr. Kennedy?" she asked.

The candidate abstractedly let her pour him a cup and started to sip it. Then suddenly he put it down. "Thank you, but I don't drink coffee," he said, and seizing his nephew's hand, he headed for the front door. In the entrance hall he seemed to feel there was something more to be said to the Sills. "Funny, I can't remember this house at all. All I remember is the family legend about my brother Joe burning down the house with his chemistry set."

Mrs. Sills smiled a chilly smile and said the house seemed to have survived it. Then the candidate said good-bye and walked out into a swelling crowd of newsmen.

As Bob Kennedy and John stepped through the door, flash bulbs exploded and newsreel cameras started to churn. These cameramen had joined the Kennedy retinue during the past ten minutes and had not received the prohibitive word—or if they had, they chose to ignore it. Kennedy looked disturbed, then shrugged philosophically, and taking John's hand, walked down the circular driveway to the street.

A group of girls in their early teens intercepted him. One asked for his autograph, and as he scrawled it, another asked, "Why did you have to leave Riverdale, Mr. Kennedy?"

A twinkle returned to the candidate's eyes. "I didn't want to leave," he said. "I was three years old at the time and I pleaded with my mother 'Why must we leave Riverdale?' But we left anyway."

The next stop on the day's itinerary was the College of Mount St. Vincent on Riverdale Avenue. A joint rally had been convened consisting of the girls from St. Vincent and the young men from nearby Manhattan College. The candidate was greeted by cheers mixed with a smattering of boos.

Kennedy climbed to the top of his car and noticed a brace of male students waving *Goldwater for President* signs. One of the boys shouted, "Go on back where you came from!"

"People have been telling me that all week," said Kennedy. "And that's why I'm here." The crowd cheered. Then Kennedy began slowly counting the Goldwater signs. "One, two, three, four, five, six—" He looked surprised. "I've been all up and down the state and that's the most Goldwater people I've seen in one place. I think they were flown in from Albany."

The crowd laughed its approval, the Goldwaterites sizzled, and the candidate leaped to the ground and steered his way toward the auditorium.

As his lithe body wove its way through the crowd of collegians, it was not difficult to picture the candidate in his college years. What had he been like? one wondered. Since a few of his classmates were members of the campaign train, an answer of sorts was not difficult to come by.

"He didn't drink or smoke," one of them said. "He did other things for a good time. Bob was not good at small talk. He was not good on social amenities. He was no great lover."

I learned he was not a reader, as was Jack. Bob Kennedy discovered books slowly at first, and then with increasing relish, finding particular appeal in history and biography.

"It was much tougher in school for him than for the others—socially, on the football field, with his studies. But he made up for it with hard work.

"On the gridiron, Bob wasn't fast, and he wasn't shifty. He had another quality—determination. It was in all his five feet, ten inches and all his hundred and sixty-five pounds. He was a quick, tough guy who worked five times as hard as anybody."

Though Kennedy was not a recluse in college, he didn't care for the frantic round of parties and dates. It had seemed to me at Le Pavillon and elsewhere that his attitude had remained much the same to this day.

Bob Kennedy's academic achievements at Harvard were average. "To tell you the truth," he once told a reporter, "I didn't go to class very much. I used to talk and argue a lot—mostly about politics."

As the candidate mounted the stage of the Mount St. Vincent auditorium, I reflected that eighteen years later he was still at it, and getting better all the time.

CHAPTER 9

The Tumult

On September 8 Robert Kennedy set out on a grueling three-day trek into Republican upstate New York. Before he returned to the relative sanctuary of Manhattan Island, he had caused an eruption of extraordinary political excitement.

In the early hours of Tuesday morning the *Caroline* had taken off from Marine Terminal and headed north for Binghamton. There was a carnival atmosphere on the plane, despite the early hour.

"It was like this in 1960," said the man from the *World-Telegram*. "The Nixon campaign train was a job. But the Kennedy train was fun. You worked your tail off, but it was a ball."

The reporters had observed that the Kennedy caravan was like the strike of lightning. For everywhere this shy, complex, and—to many at least—chilly young man went, he exercised a great emotional impact on the worshiping crowds.

"It's sex appeal," said one reporter incredulously. "He stands there, stooped and diffident, with that sad Bugs Bunny smile of his, and they love him—"

An eminent psychiatrist had put it differently. "Robert Kennedy," he said, "is the vehicle through which people can work out the grief they felt from his brother's death."

Said another, "He's the 'good father' image for the children who mob him—the young and kind father that most of us never had."

One reporter was less charitable. He was Les Whitten, crack correspondent from Hearst's Washington Bureau, on special assignment to the *New York Journal-American.*

"You know his voice is flat," said Whitten that morning as he fastened his seat belt. "It's without inflection and it's only truly like his brother's when he's hoarse."

"But his speeches, Les—" I began.

"His speeches are statistical and unimaginative."

"But his wit—" I said.

"His wit is sharp enough in private. But on the podium it's uninspired, except for a stock gag or two."

"And yet—" I said.

"I know, and yet he's a winner."

The day began with a bang in Binghamton. During a boisterous motorcade from the airport an enthusiastic crowd pulled the candidate over the back of his open convertible. But he managed to regain his footing and denied the crowd a life-size memento. They then proceeded to the Sheraton Inn, where a televised press conference was planned.

Naturally Les Whitten offered the first question. "Mr. Kennedy, what do you think of your welcome to Binghamton?"

"That's pronounced *Bing*umton, Les," said the candidate with a smile.

"I'm sorry, sir," said Whitten. "But don't forget, you've been in this state two weeks longer than I have."

The next stop was Johnson City, whose largest industry—and whose largest employer—is the Endicott Johnson Shoe Company.

"I've done two important things for the shoe industry," announced Kennedy at the town square. "First of all, eight small children need a lot of shoes. And second, I'm the one who popularized those fifty-mile hikes."

As his motorcade moved along the main street of this largely Republican city, a woman darted out of a beauty parlor, her hair a mass of curl rollers. "I just had to see him," she shouted as reporters scribbled a note. "I like that man, I really do—"

Then came Jamestown, where a commercial airliner took off during Kennedy's airport address, drowning out his voice. The candidate pointed after the jet. "He's on his way back to Phoenix to report—"

As they rolled into Jamestown, a man stood on the curb and shouted, "Go back to Massachusetts," while his wife rushed out on the highway, calling, "God bless you, Bobby!" And Jamestown was where he told an enthusiastic crowd, "I see my Long Island accent got you."

In Elmira five busloads of school children met the *Caroline*, and when they failed to quiet their shrill squeals of delight to let him speak to the crowd, the candidate said, "Now if there's any more noise I'm going to pass a law calling for school on Saturday."

One little seven-year-old girl was undeterred. "We'd still love you——" she said.

And then——Buffalo.

Our schedule had called for us to arrive at Buffalo airport at 6:05 P.M. We touched down at 8:30, with four stops still to be made in Buffalo before we slept.

Kennedy was greeted by a fantastic night scene along the ten-mile stretch from the airport to the city. It took sixty-five minutes to move that short distance.

It began with cheering crowds much like the earlier turnouts in Binghamton, Elmira, and Jamestown. But near the city of Buffalo the crowds became astonishing in their size——they were gauged to be in the tens of thousands. Seasoned reporters began shaking their heads and saying they had never seen anything like it for a Presidential candidate, let alone a Senatorial one. They had never seen it for a Rockefeller or an Eisenhower——or even a Kennedy.

As we approached the city, the tumultuous crowds were six-deep along the curb and they began to close in. Helmeted motorcycle policemen raced and backfired their engines to drive back the throngs rushing in to touch the candidate. The crowd was alive with flags, banners, placards, all lighted grotesquely by the rotating red motorcycle lights. The air was split by the sound of exploding firecrackers and the frenzied shouts of "Bobby, Bobby."

Suddenly a gray-haired woman lunged between the motorcycles like a small gray fullback, touched Kennedy's hand, and darted back, incredibly unharmed. A group of middle-aged women sprinted along the sidewalk, their spike heels clicking along the pavement. Children wove their bikes in and out among the motorcycles, perilously close to the wheels of the candidate's car.

Pink-flamed torches flared and homemade signs sprouted, reading, "RFK All the Way" and "Kennedy Next President." And shrill girlish voices echoed, "Isn't he beautiful?"

And then the cavalcade moved into the Negro district.

Now the crowds were too much for the policemen and the tone was decidedly hysterical in pitch. The mob surged through the wall of policemen, who butted them with their motorcycles but could not turn them away. They swarmed over the Kennedy car. The first wave was tumbled off as the candidate's aides pushed and shoved in a desperate attempt to keep the caravan moving. Then the second wave was turned back, in this strange battle of love and panic and politics. And through it all, the Kennedy smile was weary, the wave of the hand was somewhat tentative, and the expression was a bit surprised. A most curious sort of conquering hero . . .

After a tumultuous rally at Kleinhan's Music Hall the candidate returned to Buffalo's Hotel Statler for a few fleeting hours of sleep.

In the hotel room, Ed Guthman turned to Kennedy, who was standing by the window. "It's been quite a day," he said. "These fantastic crowds. How do you feel?"

Kennedy stared out into the night. "I keep thinking that *he* should have been doing this. These crowds should have been his—"

Robert Kennedy was up for a visit to a Westinghouse plant in nearby Cheektowaga. There in the gray half-light of morning he met the workers arriving for the 7:00 A.M. shift, shaking six hundred hands in twelve minutes, and murmuring his brief, shy greeting.

Our next stop was still another factory in the area. Here the candidate showed signs of fatigue, as though the exertions of the previous day were starting to take their toll. He stumbled over the familiar lines in his brief informal talk and his wit was less sharp than usual. But breakfast was a restorative.

We returned to the Statler Hilton for breakfast in the Terrace Room. A group of party leaders and union officials was crowded into the dining room, waiting for the candidate to address them. When he began to speak, the room grew absolutely still and all eyes were on him. All, that is, except the rather bleary eyes at the press table. They were fixed ravenously on the food. All through the candidate's remarks hands and jaws never stopped, nor did the impolite clank of silverware against chinaware. The reporters had heard this speech fifteen times in the last twenty-four hours, but none knew for certain when they would eat again. There never seemed to be enough time to eat, and this morning was no exception. Suddenly, like a weary infantry patrol responding to orders to "Move out," the correspondents tumbled away from the table. The candidate had completed his brief remarks and was heading for the door.

The *Caroline* flew on to Niagara Falls and touched down at 3:00 P.M. The candidate strode down the aisle toward the door as the reporters scampered after him. But at the end of the aisle Kennedy stopped and whirled about.

"Don't get off," said Kennedy to the surprised correspondents. "I can't stand to see your faces when I tell that joke again."

The reporters laughed.

"And I'm going to!" said the candidate, and marched down the ramp.

Several hundred people were waiting to greet him opposite the Hotel Niagara. Kennedy told the hated joke about how he had come to New York to help overtake California in population. Then he looked off into the distance. "We all know," he said, "that Niagara Falls is the greatest source of energy in America. Well, after the last thirty-six hours I could use a little help in that direction." The crowd laughed and the newsmen scribbled the improvisation. "In fact, I have given some serious thought to going over the falls in a barrel just for the rest."

The next stop was Batavia, where a delegation of six girls from the nearby town of Kennedy was waiting.

"You see?" said Kennedy. "They talk about my being a carpetbagger and I even have a *city* named after me."

The crowds seemed to grow in ferocity and size as the day wore on. In Batavia the candidate had to jump from one car to another to get to his own, and finally fell into the rear of his vehicle to escape the muscular affection of his fans. And a little later the exuberance of his admirers turned into a mob scene during which his chin was cut and bleeding.

By now Kennedy's aides—Guthman, Markham, and King—had improvised security procedures and were doubling in brass as bodyguards.

Markham and King rode the rear deck of Kennedy's car. When he stopped to greet onlookers, the two would hold him by the belt and legs to keep him from being yanked into the crowd by handshakers. It was a precaution that was not always successful, and the candidate was more than once catapulted into space by the affectionate well-wishers. Nor could they protect the candidate's hands from the onslaught of love. His knuckles were by now beet-red and his hands were scraped and bruised.

Kennedy himself was the architect of much of the chaos that enveloped him. In his search for votes he encouraged the crowd by reaching out to shake their hands. Though he could have easily instructed the police to guarantee an easy passage, this would not have produced votes—particularly for a candidate who was trying to demolish an image as a cold, power-hungry politician.

Then came the towns of LeRoy and Caledonia in rural Livingstone County. LeRoy and Caledonia, where no Democrat for major office had campaigned since 1948. LeRoy and Caledonia, where the Republican enrollment was two-to-one or better.

So in LeRoy a frantic woman snatched a tuft of Kennedy's hair right out of his head, and a teen-ager repeated the assault as the candidate gritted his teeth in pain and Ed Guthman yanked the youngster's hand away.

And in Caledonia six frantic handshakers fought for his hand and nearly pulled him off the speaker's platform before his aides wrestled his body away from them.

Save him from his friends, I thought as I watched from the safety of the press bus. No one except possibly the Beatles seemed to stir such frenzy as Bob Kennedy. And, astonishingly, here in the rock-ribbed Republican belt the response had bordered on the hysterical.

Around his slight body was the aura of the fallen leader. The crowds, I reflected, see him as the devoted brother who stood in service at the side of Jack Kennedy, through the struggles, the triumphs, and the tragedy.

And then, of course, there was "his goddamn sex appeal," as one reporter put it with a mixture of envy and incredulity. There was this shy, diffident young man with the unmistakable appeal to women.

But among the screamers there were also the doubters. There were doubts about the candidate's character—was he too ambitious and too ruthless and too zealous? The doubters sympathized with the white-haired Senator Keating—and he appeared white-haired in every sense of the word. For Kenneth Keating was the underdog, fighting on his own home ground against a man who lacked even the right to vote for himself in the coming election.

So Robert Kennedy continued to endure and invite the onslaughts of public affection. For though amid the clamorous welcomes there was no sign of a ground swell of resentment, no one doubted for a minute that it was there.

The last stop on the second day was Rochester—home town of Senator Kenneth Keating.

Nothing, I thought, could impress me after the volcanic reception in Buffalo the night before. The reporters were swearing never again to file a story headlining the mammoth mobs.

"If I send in one more story about the unprecedented crowds," said Johnny Apple of the *Times,* "my editor will crown me."

"Mine's the same way," said Frank Lynn of the *Telegram.* "They ought to be out here. It's hard to visualize this unless you're here."

And, of course, Rochester outdid them all.

A wild crowd of forty thousand was waiting as the Kennedy motorcade rolled into town. There was little in the reception to convince the candidate that he was in enemy territory. The birthplace and residence of the Republican incumbent was putting on a dazzling welcome.

A reporter from a Rochester newspaper was emphatic. "It's the biggest turnout since Jack Kennedy came here in 1960."

The route took us through a predominantly Irish-Catholic neighborhood and within five blocks of the scene of the nation's worst racial riots the month before. In the Negro section, Rochester's Third Ward, Kennedy received his most tumultuous greeting. Enthusiastic handshakers pulled him almost into the street before Markham and King won the bizarre tug-of-war. Then four Negro youths managed to climb on the Kennedy car and had to be pulled off by security guards.

Through the tumult the motorcade wended its way— first the motorcycles, then the busload of Kennedy Girls, a police car, a convertible overflowing with photographers, the candidate's open car, his aides, another police car, and the lumbering press bus, bullying its way through the crush.

As we approached the Sheraton Hotel in downtown Rochester, the throng filled the sidewalks and street and struggled to break through the police lines. The candidate, three hours behind on his schedule, climbed to the hood of his car, raised an electric megaphone to his mouth, and thanked the crowd for their greeting.

"There's nothing like a quiet evening in Rochester," he said dryly.

In his hotel suite Kennedy had a moment to catch his breath and gather his thoughts for the speech at the Rochester Civic Center, where four thousand Rochesterians had been waiting for three hours. A local political leader was in the apartment and offered a word of advice. "I wouldn't mention civil rights or the race thing if I were you, Bob. Most people here are pretty bitter about those riots—"

The candidate frowned a Jovian frown and disappeared into the bathroom, where a tub of boiling water awaited him.

So great was the melee outside the Rochester Civic Center that it took a flying wedge of thirty policemen to take the candidate the forty feet from the street to the entrance. Two young women, one of them hysterical, fainted in the crush and were hauled away by the police.

Once inside, Kennedy took the stage and began his extemporaneous speech by exploiting a fact he had picked up from the fact sheet.

"It gives me a deep sense of satisfaction to come here to Rochester, since I know it is the home town of a distinguished white-haired American . . ." The crowd laughed appreciatively. "And I am referring, of course, to Susan B. Anthony."

Then the candidate launched into his almost ritualistic speech on the problems of New York, the accomplishments of his brother's administration, and the need for at least one Democratic Senator to work with a Democratic administration.

The audience applauded their agreement. Standing at the foot of the stage, I saw an expression of doubt race over the candidate's face, to be replaced by one of resolution.

"It would have been easier," he said, "not to try to bring this matter up, but there are problems we are all going to have to face. I'm referring to the problem of the races living together."

The audience was stonily silent.

"In the South you can pass legislation to permit a Negro to have an ice cream cone at Howard Johnson's, but you *can't* pass legislation to automatically give a Negro an *education*. I believe the community must provide education so there can be *jobs*."

The applause started weakly in the back, then it grew and spread across the auditorium.

"You have got," said the candidate, "to give Negroes some *hope*."

The last day of our three-day odyssey began with another predawn factory visit. But the press had had enough of trying to keep up with the candidate's rigorous timetable. They had a plan.

The previous day several weary reporters had caucused on the press bus and conspired to send one of their number on the pre-breakfast stops the following morning. The luckless journalist, it was agreed, would cover the events and at breakfast would provide the others with the details, enabling them to file their stories.

"After all," said one correspondent, "he won't say anything new. And he'll just tell that lousy joke again."

So the following morning, when the candidate paid a 6:00 A.M. visit to Rochester's Delco plant, he did so without a full press contingent. And shameful to admit, he did so without me as well.

A long day stretched ahead of him. His schedule called for eighteen speeches, eight airplane hops, and visits to six counties before he wound up his day at his Glen Cove home at midnight. The schedule *called* for his homecoming at midnight, but events dictated otherwise.

The Kennedy cavalcade swept through Oswego, Watertown, and Ogdensburg. And then on to Massena.

In Massena the candidate noticed that signs reading "Welcome Ted Kennedy" had been converted to "Welcome Bob Kennedy" by the simple expedient of a bit of pasteboard and a stapler. The signs had originally awaited Ted Kennedy the night his plane crashed when he was on his way to speak in Massena.

Kennedy tore the word "Bob" from one of the signs and held it up to the crowd. "There's one big advantage to electing me," he said. "It will be cheaper for everybody. We can interchange signs with Massachusetts—"

Night was falling as the *Caroline* set down at Adirondack Airport and the motorcade sped through the resort areas of Saranac Lake and Lake Placid. The crowds were large and responsive, but Kennedy's aides were growing concerned about how far they had fallen behind schedule.

In downtown Plattsburgh their doubts were momentarily assuaged when six thousand people swarmed around the candidate at a bridge dedication. Kennedy marched through the pressing mob in virtual darkness. The flashes of the cameras had created a "false dawn" effect that triggered photoelectric cells and automatically turned off all the street lights!

So the candidate said his few words lighted by the demonic bursts of flash bulbs, and then fought his way back to his white convertible.

"He's exhausted, let him through," shouted a teenager as her girl friend grabbed for him. The candidate, his lips slack with fatigue, waved at the well-wishers and entered his car for the drive to the Plattsburgh Airport.

On the *Caroline*, Kennedy spooned tomato soup as the plane took off for the thirty-minute flight to Glens Falls. The schedule called for arrival there at 8:00 P.M. It was now 1:00 A.M. and the candidate was distressed at having disappointed the residents of that city.

"What time is it?" said the candidate.

"We're five hours late," said Ed Guthman dourly.

"Do you think anybody waited?"

As the *Caroline* touched down at Glens Falls Airport, the press corps produced an anemic smattering of applause for the pilot, the ramp was lowered, and the candidate appeared at the open door. As he did so the sound of three brass bands split the night air and a full-bodied roar went up from a thousand throats.

They had waited in the dark for five hours. Many had gone home for dinner, put the children in pajamas, and returned to their vigil—with the children. Flash bulbs lighted the candidate's drawn face as the crowds broke onto the runway to greet him. Kennedy gulped mightily and hopped aboard the hood of an available auto.

"Thank you for waiting," he said, and he seemed to have trouble finding the words. Then he broke into a grin. "Well, here we are five hours late. That's the well-oiled Kennedy machine for you."

The motorcade finally moved away from the airport and through the night streets of the city. Women in nightgowns lined the curb, men in T-shirts and slacks, children in pajamas. Then suddenly we rounded a corner and there were five thousand people—a third of the population of Glens Falls.

The candidate struggled through the darkness and mounted a platform to deafening cheers. Finally, after a very long time, the cheers died.

"I'd like," he said, "to make my very first commitment of the campaign. I promise that win or lose, the day after election day, I'm coming back to Glens Falls."

And so he did.

CHAPTER 10

[×]

The City

As Robert Kennedy labored through his triumphal up-state tour, his "advance men" were cautiously surveying the metropolitan boroughs of Brooklyn and Manhattan.

It is the function of an advance man to detail the precise route that the candidate's motorcade will travel. He must make sure there will be sufficient time for movement from place to place, from rally to rally. When the candidate arrived in Glens Falls five hours late, it was felt that the upstate advance men had been too prodigal with Mr. Kennedy's appointments and his schedule had been unrealistically overcrowded.

No one, of course, had anticipated the enormous crowds that played havoc with the clock, making it impossible to move from Rally A to Reception B in the time allotted.

"You know," said Kennedy's press secretary, Debs Myers, "I've known lots of candidates who could stay on schedule every single day. It's easy. All it takes is good planning and massive public indifference."

• • •

There was increasing concern in the Kennedy camp about the votes in metropolitan New York. Normally the Democratic candidate could leave New York City with a healthy plurality which hopefully would offset a heavy upstate deficit. But this was a curious campaign. Kennedy showed surprising strength upstate, while there was talk of major defections in New York City.

In troubled late-night conferences Kennedy strategists argued persuasively for the candidate to spend more time in New York City. So on a bright Sunday morning Robert Kennedy, accompanied by his wife and his husky eleven-year-old son, Joseph, set out on what the mimeographed schedule optimistically called "a walking tour."

On the drive from the Carlyle to the kickoff point, the subject had turned to literature.

"What book would you say influenced you the most, Mrs. Kennedy?" asked a reporter.

"Oh dear," said Ethel, "after Ian Fleming, what?"

Little Joe came to attention. "I just finished a James Bond mystery," he said, "and I can't wait to read another one—"

"You just keep on with *The Imitation of Christ*," said Ethel Kennedy decisively. Then she looked at the back of Joseph's head and frowned at the curly tangle. "He's got hair like his father. Has anybody got a comb?"

The walking tour began at Broadway and 90th Street. It rapidly turned into a shoving tour.

The police came well prepared, in number and paraphernalia. There were more than a hundred of them, with half a dozen mounted patrolmen. They were equipped with walkie-talkies, bull horns, and other riot control devices. And they needed every bit of it. Surging crowds pushed forward against the police lines to shake the candidate's hand as the little band proceeded intrepidly down the west side of Broadway. Wooden barricades had been placed along the route, but the thousands of New Yorkers threatened to overrun them at a dozen points. When Kennedy reached 88th Street we heard a loud, sharp report. Police moved quickly to the source of the explosion, beneath the marquee of a motion picture theatre. Their investigation turned up fragments of a firecracker, tossed by some prankster with a psychopathic streak.

Kennedy moved tenaciously down Broadway, bringing all the fervor and excitement to "sophisticated" New York City that he had been generating elsewhere in the state. Young Joe, dressed in his Ivy League best, was smiling bravely in the teeth of the pedestrian onslaught.

"What do you think of campaigning?" I shouted to him.

"It's sort of fun," he said doubtfully.

At 87th Street an elderly woman shouted, "Let him go back to Massachusetts! Let him go back to Virginia! We're nothing to him but a stepping stone!"

Three determined women wheeled in on her.

"Shut up, stupid, I love him!" shouted the first.

"I came from Philadelphia, so we're *all* carpetbaggers!" shrieked another.

"Go hide in a closet!" shouted a third, somewhat irrelevantly.

The elderly woman glowered impotently and drifted away into the crowd.

A teen-age boy came darting out of the crowd through the cordon of police. "Forget about the signature, just touch my autograph book," he pleaded. The candidate obliged him with the curious benediction.

As he touched the book I noticed the candidate's hand was quite puffy and the gray worsted suit that had lain so freshly pressed across his bed that morning was now badly wrinkled from the crush.

"You're taking quite a beating," I said.

The candidate shrugged stoically. "I need the exercise."

Kennedy continued his forced march southward. Women rushed up to put headlocks on him and solidly buss his cheek. Children came running after him in a frenzy. Men elbowed their way to his side to lock eyes with him and say, "Good luck."

At 86th Street the press of the crowds threatened to become unmanageable and the candidate asked me to take his wife out of the line of march.

"Think of all the fun you're missing because of—uh —your condition," I said as we headed for a closed car.

"My condition!" she said. "Why is it that the English language is so poor that we have no graceful way of saying that someone is expecting a child?"

Once in the car we glanced out at the surging throng. "Well," I said, "at least this campaign keeps you from getting bored."

"Boredom," said Ethel Kennedy, "has never been a problem with us."

I could believe her. I looked at this vivid, informal, spontaneous young woman and thought of the photos I had seen of her—horseback riding, playing tennis, touring Japan, playing touch football, skiing . . .

"You met Bob on a skiing trip, didn't you?"

"Yes, it was up at Mont Tremblant near Quebec. Bobby was momentarily mad about me."

"Understandable."

"He took me out for two weeks. The only trouble was that for the next two years he took out my older sister."

"Well," I said, "I consider his major achievement in life—after civil rights and the Cuban crisis—was marrying you."

"It certainly took him long enough to decide," said Ethel Kennedy.

The next stop was Brooklyn.

Brooklyn was important because of its large Democratic Jewish population. Polls had shown a massive potential defection of Jewish voters, and this had transformed the race from a probable runaway to an uncomfortably close contest.

Keating's courtship of New York Jewry—his anti-Arab utterances, his attendance at weddings and bar mitzvahs—had borne fruit. And so, in an attempt to recapture the so-called Jewish vote, Robert Kennedy was driving himself on a back-breaking regimen to show that descriptions of him as a ruthless monster were somewhat exaggerated.

At stake was more than the future of Robert Kennedy. There was also the future of both the parties in

New York State—and there were the clear implications on the national scene.

So the Kennedy motorcade swung through Brooklyn and the sometimes smiling, sometimes solemn candidate addressed himself to the task of conquering the minority groups that made of the borough an ethnic quilt.

As the cavalcade moved, shouting, shoving, surging people slowed it to a crawl and nearly overpowered it, like some invading horde armed with love. The sacred Sunday-morning silence of the Borough of Churches was shattered by ear-splitting sirens and loudspeakers proclaiming the coming of the candidate. Sunday motorists stared astounded, teen-agers raced along, and housewives were drawn from their Sunday dishes and came rushing into the street, shouting, "Bobby!"

At one point Kennedy had gone back to sit in the press bus when suddenly he spied a crowd of third-grade schoolchildren on the curb. Kennedy ordered the bus to stop and headed for the door.

"Come on," he called back to the reporters. "These are my people—"

When the group of youngsters had clustered about him, Kennedy raised his voice in mock solemnity.

"If I am elected I promise to shorten the school term . . ."

Cheers.

". . . and lengthen the school day."

Groans.

Then the dazzling Kennedy smile.

The children that so often surrounded Kennedy served a purpose far beyond that of enlarging the crowd and

enhancing the excitement. They also helped to destroy
the image of Robert Kennedy as a merciless prosecuting
attorney. The candidate showed a natural warmth in
dealing with children and a genuine concern lest they
be injured in the crush that surrounded him. And adults
—particularly women—could not help noticing how
children took an immediate liking to this ruthless fellow.

Kennedy's forehead was etched with fatigue as his
motorcade headed for Coney Island and the famous
frankfurter emporium called Nathan's. Coney Island
had not seen such tumult since the Brooklyn Dodgers
left for Los Angeles.

"Did any of you," he asked the crowd, "know that Mr.
Nathan's last name is Hamburgher?"

There was no response, not even from the polite few
in the crowd who must have known Mr. Nathan's last
name was Handwerker.

"See?" said Kennedy. "You have to be a real New
Yorker to know that."

The candidate accepted an enormous bag of frank-
furters for his children from Mr. Hamburgher and then
washed down a mustard-soaked hot dog with a paper cup
of beer. In between bites he asked Frank Lynn of the
World-Telegram if he would be going upstate with him
the following week.

"No," said Lynn. "I'm going to be in Boston, of all
places."

"Never heard of it," said Kennedy.

By dusk the candidate had met Catholics, Jews, Negroes,
Puerto Ricans, shaking hands with virtually every large

minority—except Protestants. He had invaded every corner of New York's most populous borough. Tens of thousands had seen him. His car had picked its way, barely moving, through screaming crowds packed doorfront to door-front. At one stop, beneath the elevated lines of the BMT subway, a crowd of mature women were near hysteria as they screamed for the touch of his hand.

"It's like something out of O'Neill," said Les Whitten.

"O'Neill?" I said.

"Desire under the Els," said Whitten.

Politicians who had made a career of convoying candidates through the gray streets of Brooklyn swore they had never witnessed such a tempestuous reception. In traveling about New York, the white-haired Kenneth Keating had enjoyed fairly good receptions. But Robert Kennedy had destroyed the modest standards of *all* Senatorial candidates.

As columnist Murray Kempton observed, "There has come into Mr. Keating's eyes trouble that was never there before, and it has to embody the pain of no longer being able to look at an ordinary crowd without thinking how extraordinary Robert Kennedy's would be . . ."

Wherever Kennedy went in Brooklyn, the reaction was the same—police barricades were flattened, children were knocked down, the candidate was trapped in the center of turbulence. Always there was the shrill chant of "We want Bobby," the screams for a touch of his hand, the near-hysteria of children, the schoolgirlish behavior of mature women.

I noticed one who was quietly wandering along the rear echelon of the crowd, apparently scouting for a better vantage point from which to view the candidate. Since I was wearing a *Kennedy Press* button, I decided to exploit it for intelligence purposes.

"Has the candidate's speech affected the way you'll vote?" I asked.

"No," she said decisively, "he didn't persuade me to change my vote." She clasped her shopping bag more protectively. "But I think he'll probably pick up a lot of votes among the masses."

The Commercial

That first day I had come to the Kennedy apartment, the Attorney General was considering whether to accept an invitation to appear on *Meet the Press* that very Sunday. He had decided to wait until the campaign was further along and the issues were crystalized. Now seven weeks later that day had arrived. At 6:00 P.M. Robert Kennedy would go under the Lawrence Spivak scalpel, "live" from the NBC studios at Rockefeller Center.

Early that afternoon a curious meeting was convened on the front lawn of Gracie Mansion. Its purpose was to permit a group of men to hurl at the candidate some of the questions that might be asked him by the *Meet the Press* panel. Gracie Mansion is the official residence of the Mayor of the City of New York. Its exterior has all the charm of a rest home for the aged, and its lawn, stretching out to the East River, has the matted look of a public parade ground. All in all, something less than one might expect for the chief executive of the world's largest city.

We carried some metal chairs down from the porch onto the grass and pulled them into a circle, like covered wagons seeking protection from an Indian raid. At one end of the flattened circle, facing into the sun as usual, sat Robert Kennedy in a pale green pullover and khaki trousers. Ranged around him from left to right—in a directional sense—were Arthur Schlesinger, Jr., former Presidential aide and historian; Jimmy Wechsler, columnist for the *New York Post*; Ed Guthman, the candidate's closest aide; Bill vandenHeuvel and Milt Gwirtzman, his chief speechwriters; and Bernie Ruggieri, astute aide to Mayor Wagner, on loan to the candidate.

Schlesinger had flown in expressly for this briefing. *Meet the Press's* large viewing audience was expected to be even larger due to Kennedy's appearance, so the program could either be helpful or damaging in a race that had grown extremely close.

"All right," said the candidate, squinting into the sun, "fire away."

For the next two hours Kennedy was assaulted by every form of loaded and devious question one could conceive. Sometimes he would ask for facts to support an answer. Sometimes he would merely snap, "I can handle that," and move on to the next.

One question thrown by Jimmy Wechsler was difficult to field and stopped the meeting in its tracks. Someone suggested a possible answer.

"But that's a lie," said Kennedy simply.

At about 3:00 P.M. the questions—and the questioners—were exhausted and the candidate left for the Carlyle and an hour's nap. Schlesinger, vandenHeuvel, and I left the mansion's grounds in search of a restaurant. It had been a long morning and none of us had had any lunch.

· · ·

In the *Meet the Press* studio, out of range of the cameras, were three rows of bridge chairs for observers. They were nearly all filled with members of the Kennedy press entourage. It struck me there was something superfluous about reporters covering *other* reporters questioning a candidate.

Under the antiseptic gleam of the overhead lights sat the three guest journalists, looking oddly lifeless, and off to one side, looking like an amiable gray Satan, sat Lawrence Spivak.

At a few minutes of the hour—why did he always cut these things so fine?—Robert Kennedy entered the studio, accompanied by his wife. Spivak rose to greet them, Mrs. Kennedy took a seat in the front row of the observers' rank, and Mr. Kennedy took the hot seat opposite camera number one.

The clock ticked inexorably around. Finally a tiny red light flashed on atop one of the cameras and we were on the air.

As the red second hand swept along, the candidate fielded questions with skill, if with a certain lack of zest. But if he failed to show the warmth he exhibited on the stump, neither did he provide support for the ruthless image. It was also satisfying to see that not one of the more difficult questions that had been anticipated at Gracie Mansion was propounded by the panel. Which provides an example of Kennedy methods: prepare for the worst and everything will be downhill.

Only one question seemed to give the candidate pause.

"I asked this of Senator Keating," said Spivak

hoarsely. "Now I'd like to ask it of you. For what do you think you will be remembered?"

Kennedy stared at the unblinking eye of the TV camera as the seconds ticked away. Good Lord, I thought, considering the activities of the man in the Justice Department, on the Rackets Committee, as adviser to the President—

"I'm sorry I didn't know you asked Mr. Keating that—" he began haltingly.

"I *gave* him a transcript of the Keating interview!" Bill vandenHeuvel whispered somewhere behind me.

"I suppose," began Kennedy, "I'd like to be remembered for my activities in behalf of human rights, and the confrontation with the Russians over their missiles in Cuba—"

How very like Robert Kennedy, I thought. That's just the sort of question he would have difficulty in answering, simply because he doesn't think that way. He's probably never once given a thought to the things for which he "will be remembered." He thinks less about his place in history than of this morning's problems that history has dumped on his desk . . .

Meet the Press ground on and finally the little red light winked out and the On the Air sign went black. Mr. and Mrs. Robert Kennedy rose and walked to one another, and a smiling Mr. Spivak moved in to make it a convivial triangle.

Ethel Kennedy took Spivak's arm familiarly. "You know, you're not *nearly* as mean as they say."

"Bob, I'd like you to come on the show again the week **after** the election," said Spivak, which seemed to imply that Larry Spivak, at least, had made up his mind who would be the next U.S. Senator from New York.

"Fine," said Kennedy, "fine."

Spivak saw the Kennedys to the elevator and we descended to the lobby of 30 Rockefeller Plaza.

Jim King was waiting at the curb with the candidate's car. "Come on," said Kennedy, "we're going to see a TV commercial." Then he and his wife climbed in the back seat and King headed the car toward the Videotape Center.

"I thought that went well," said Ethel.

"I didn't do too well with that question about why I have a reputation for being ruthless," said Kennedy.

"You handled it better when Charles Collingwood asked you that on *CBS Reports*," said Ethel.

"What did he tell Charles Collingwood?" said King.

"He said that as Attorney General he had been engaged in struggles involving civil rights and organized crime. And before that he had been involved in struggles with corrupt union leaders. He said these were difficult struggles and he pursued them vigorously, and that some people might have gotten the impression he was ruthless from that."

"I'm convinced," said King.

"Mr. Spivak seemed positively bland," said Ethel.

"It might have been better if he was tougher," said the candidate. "It's the *difficult* questions that let you talk about the things people have on their minds."

On the way to the Videotape Center, Kennedy decided to drop in on his 42nd Street headquarters. He climbed the wooden stairs to the makeshift office of Joe Dolan, a former Justice Department aide who was acting as liaison with the ad agency.

On the wall of Dolan's small cubicle were a great many preliminary layouts of campaign literature.

"How many fliers do we have in use?" said Kennedy.

"Three," said Dolan.

"How many layouts are in preparation?"

"Thirty-eight."

Kennedy was appalled. "Another week and you won't have to print anything. You can hand out the *layouts*."

"The problem," explained Dolan, "is that everybody is always tinkering. They keep tinkering and things get rewritten and delayed."

"Never mind that. Let's get something *out*. What's this?" Kennedy pointed to a layout that contained testimonials to the candidate by various public figures.

"That's a flier for handing out at rallies."

"Forget the testimonials. This flier should tell where I stand on key issues. Change it."

"You're tinkering," said Dolan.

"Change it," said Kennedy.

The car pulled up in front of the Videotape Center on Columbus Avenue. A young man led the way to a private viewing room where several people were waiting for the candidate's arrival.

Jacqueline Kennedy was there, looking composed and wearing her small quizzical smile. Brother-in-law Steve Smith was there, looking lean, boyish and immaculately dressed. And ad agency chief Fred Papert was there with several members of his staff.

Papert's original idea for television advertising—putting Kennedy in small crowds, on street corners and in supermarkets, and having him respond to questions from them—was disappointing.

In the framework of one-minute television commercials, the candidate's answers sounded glib, hurried, curiously unconvincing. In attempting to compress his views on a given problem to forty-five seconds, the Kennedy qualities of grace and spontaneity seemed to be lost.

However, the filming of these one-minute "spots" did produce one wildly memorable moment that took several years from Debs Myers' life.

"The agency," Myers recalled, "suggested we film one of these things on the Staten Island Ferry. So there we were, out in the middle of the river at eight A.M., about to start shooting. Suddenly I notice the ferry's turning around and heading back to shore. The passengers are furious because they'll be late for work. The newspaper boys are asking me what's happening—"

"What *was* happening?" I said.

"The agency was trying to get the Statue of Liberty behind the candidate."

"What you're about to see," said Papert, when everyone in the screening room was comfortably seated, "is a thirty-minute television commercial. It was edited from ninety minutes' worth of footage we filmed at Columbia University last week."

I recalled the occasion well.

The Columbia gymnasium had been crowded with undergraduates, waiting impatiently for the candidate's arrival. Campaign Manager Steve Smith sat at a ringside seat smiling benignly and fielding questions propounded by a reporter from the university newspaper.

Lem Billings and Fred Papert—the two men responsible for campaign advertising—checked microphones and camera angles.

And outside four hundred students, for whom there was no room in the overcrowded gymnasium, waited to greet the candidate—with catcalls or cheers, according to their advocacy.

Finally the candidate arrived, shook the outstretched hands of cheerers and catcallers alike, entered the hall, and strode to the microphone at center stage.

He did not make a speech, but instead opened the program to questions—and then three TV cameras positioned around the room began to churn.

And now, in a windowless screening room on Columbus Avenue, Kennedy would view the commercial made from that film.

The lights in the viewing room flickered out and all eyes were on the screen in the corner. Suddenly the door swung open and a blond head projected into the room. It was actress Shelley Winters, Democrat, liberal, casuist supreme. She was filming a television play elsewhere in the building. "Hello," she said uncertainly. "How's it going?" Then she noticed the viewing screen. "Oops, I'm sorry. I didn't mean to interrupt. If there's anything I can do, just let me know." With that the door swung shut and our attention returned to the screen.

The questions were tough, almost embarrassingly so. And each time Kennedy retrieved them, using them as springboards to make his points.

There was even a healthy leavening of humor. At one point a questioner asked, "What is your position on birth control?" Ethel Kennedy, who was seated at the side of the hall, promptly got up and headed for the door.

The half-hour finally ended.

"What do you think?" said the candidate.

"I think it's good," said Steve Smith. "I think it's damn good."

"What do you think, Jackie?" said the candidate.

"Oh, I think it was splendid, don't you?" she said in her breathless voice.

"Yes, I guess so," said the candidate.

"You used the same quotation twice," said Ed Guthman. "The one about our having the power to make this the best generation or the last."

"Too late to do anything about it," said Papert. "These films are already in the hands of stations all over the state."

Someone entered the room to report that a party named Debs Myers was on the phone and was anxious to speak to Kennedy. He and Smith went to one of the deserted offices.

"What is it, Debs?" said the candidate, as Steve Smith listened on an extension.

"Keating has just issued a statement accusing you of running an arrogant, insulting, and juvenile campaign that demonstrates you are constitutionally unfit to be a Senator."

"He's on to you," said Smith wryly.

"I think you should issue a statement," said Myers

without amusement. This was the daily crisis that landed on Myers' desk every evening with unfailing regularity.

"I don't think we should dignify it with an answer," said the candidate and hung up.

Steve Smith smiled at his brother-in-law. "Mr. Keating is getting desperate," he said.

CHAPTER 12

The First Lady

A few evenings later a staff meeting was held at the Carlyle. Kennedy had been invited to appear on most of the major radio and TV interview shows, and the purpose of the meeting was to decide which of them would best serve his candidacy.

After the merits of various shows were considered and final selections made, Tom Costigan, the nattily dressed, red-faced man who was in charge of TV and radio commitments, reminded the candidate of his appearance the following morning on the *Today Show*, an early-morning television show with a large following.

"Most of the audience are women," said Costigan. "It would be very helpful if your wife could join you."

Ethel was in McLean, Virginia, with the children, and the candidate phoned her there. She agreed to fly to New York early the following morning for the program. When Kennedy hung up the phone he looked dispirited.

"It isn't easy for Ethel these days," he said. "Driving all the kids to school. She says she's in a car pool now. She doesn't have the Attorney General's limousine and chauffeur any more."

Costigan and the others finally gathered up their papers, said their goodnights, and filed out. As I started for the door, Kennedy took me aside. "Would you like to join Mrs. Kennedy and me for dinner downstairs?"

"I'd be happy to," I said, suddenly puzzled how Ethel Kennedy could have traveled from Virginia to the Carlyle in twenty minutes. "I'll be down in a few minutes," I said, and phoned the Kennedy press office about one final bit of unfinished business.

As a tribute to my perception, I must say that it was well before the elevator disgorged me in the lobby that I realized just which Mrs. Kennedy I was to be dining with.

In the dimly lit lounge of the Carlyle, I asked where Robert Kennedy was seated and was shown to a table in the corner. There, behind an upholstered pillar, sat Jacqueline Bouvier Kennedy.

The candidate introduced us and she extended a hand and a warm smile. "How do you do?"

There was an abundance of suggestions on ways in which Jacqueline Kennedy could be used in the campaign. They included everything from television commercials to joining the candidate at Mass at St. Patrick's Cathedral.

He said no to all of them.

"I'm sorry I didn't get to go to the Bronx the other night," she said. Jacqueline Kennedy had planned to join Pat Lawford, Kennedy's sister, as an anonymous observer at a series of rallies in the Bronx a few evenings before. But the plan had come a cropper when Mrs. Lawford begged off with a headache.

"I've been shopping for a wig that would provide enough concealment to let me watch from the crowd."

"You could try a turban," said the candidate. "They provide very good camouflage."

"Perhaps," said Mrs. Kennedy doubtfully. "I *would* like to see you campaigning. Have the crowds been friendly?"

"Well, there was one little boy in Watertown," said Kennedy, "who wasn't especially friendly. He was carrying a large sign that read, 'Don't use *me* in your cynical power grab.' "

"What did you say?" asked Jacqueline Kennedy.

"I promised I wouldn't," said Robert Kennedy.

Mrs. Kennedy laughed.

"I remember another sign in Jamestown," said the candidate. "A little boy holding a sign reading, 'Bobby Goldberg is for Bobby Kennedy.' And standing next to him was another boy with a sign reading, 'Bobby Ryan isn't.' "

"It must be a terrible burden to be smiling at great crowds of people all day long," I said.

"It's not bad," said the candidate.

"Of course, you know what you *could* do," said Mrs. Kennedy. "You could turn on a very low level smile. It's the really broad smiles that tire you out. A gentle little smile would wear better."

"You mean something like this?" said Kennedy, and produced a villainous smirk.

Mrs. Kennedy laughed appreciatively.

"Or perhaps something more like this," said the candidate, and flashed a frightened little smile—the look of a man watching the dentist's pincers closing in.

"On second thought," said Jacqueline Kennedy thoughtfully, "I think you'd better stay with the full smile."

In the lounge of the Carlyle there were other entertainments besides Kennedy-watching. There was a continental pianist named George Feyer, of whose style one could justly and charitably say it was unobtrusive.

At one point in the evening, Feyer approached the table, bowed in a courtly fashion to the former First Lady, smiled benignly, and said, "Such a great pleasure to have you with us this evening, Mrs. Kennedy."

Jacqueline Kennedy murmured an acknowledgment.

Then M. Feyer bowed again, and in the tone of a man bestowing a great gift, said, "Would you mind if I played some music from *Camelot?*"

Mrs. Kennedy smiled her most radiant smile. "Yes, I would," she said.

M. Feyer's face crumpled and he bowed himself away.

Next a waiter descended on our table, bearing a menu inscribed with a lengthy message for Mrs. Kennedy from a fellow diner. She read it, smiled, laid it aside, and resumed her conversation.

A few minutes later a woman bore down on the table, snatched up the menu, stared vengefully at Mrs. Kennedy, and stalked back to her table.

"What was that all about?" said the candidate.

On the heels of this understanding soul came a heavy-set man with the sheen of commercial success on his suit and his jowls. He advanced on the table, seized Bob Kennedy's hand, returned it to him with reluctance, and said, "Please excuse the intrusion—I did want to wish you the best of luck in your campaign. But I didn't want to intrude on your privacy. Please forgive—"

Then he turned his importuning on Mrs. Kennedy. "I pray you'll excuse the intrusion, but I had to tell you the great affection and sympathy we feel for you. But please forgive the intrusion—" And with that, he began to back away. "Intrusion—forgive—forgive—" And he extruded his way back to his table.

Bob Kennedy signed the check, and before handing it to the waiter, extended it to his sister-in-law. "Did you ever see such an awful handwriting?" he said in amazement, as though seeing it for the first time.

"It *is* pretty bad," she conceded.

Robert Kennedy's handwriting is cramped in the fashion of a small boy's, with all the letters elbowing one another for breathing space.

"Today I had to send a sample of my handwriting to a handwriting analyst to appraise in her syndicated column. Angie asked me to write a sentence as a specimen."

"What did you write?" asked Mrs. Kennedy.

" 'If you tell your readers what you see in my handwriting, you'll cost me the election,' " said the candidate.

Whereupon Robert Kennedy and Mrs. John Kennedy rose and headed for the door.

As they walked toward the exit, all conversation in the room suddenly ceased, and there was the unmistakable feeling that royalty had left its box and was returning to the palace.

CHAPTER 13

The Taping

The next week was an extraordinary one. The Republican party failed to buy up the time of *That Was the Week That Was*. So as its chief writer, I had a television show to do.

The first time they had pre-empted us, the GOP used the time to present a filmed conversation between Dwight Eisenhower and Barry Goldwater at the farm in Gettysburg. The show brought us an enthusiastic letter.

> *What a wonderful coup for TW3—presenting those two aging comedians. Keep up the good work.*

But this week we were on the air and a script had been prepared based on the happenings of the last seven days. One of the pieces in the show involved the Pierre Salinger—George Murphy race in California. Thinking that Salinger might enjoy watching the spoof, I sent him the following wire:

> DEAR PIERRE. I THINK YOU WILL GET A KICK OUT OF WHAT YOU SEE OVER NBC-TV AT 9:30 TUESDAY NIGHT. BEST,
>
> GERALD GARDNER

So early Tuesday morning, former President Herbert Hoover died and NBC pre-empted our time to present a memorial program.

The network's decision reached us at the NBC studio on Tuesday afternoon just as our final rehearsals were getting under way. The cast was understandably disturbed over the cancellation. For three consecutive weeks we were snatched from the air to be replaced by GOP commercials. Now we were to be undone by the passing of a Republican statesman. It seemed to be part of one great conspiracy.

Leland Hayward, the program's producer, had been weathering crises ever since Mary Martin complained the nightly shampooing in *South Pacific* was ruining her hair. So he accepted the news with equanimity. "How's Bobby's campaign going?" he asked.

"The polls show him sliding," I said. "Did you see him on *Meet the Press?*"

He made a face. "That was a catastrophe. He was so solemn. You ought to let me talk to him before he does anything else for television."

"I will," I said.

Ed Guthman called that evening to say the candidate wanted to deliver a five-minute speech on TV to explain why he wanted to be a Senator. He had dictated an outline of his thoughts and wanted me to put them in final form. There was plenty of time. A studio had been reserved for the following morning.

Kennedy's draft, dictated ad lib to Angie Novello was

quite close to a final product. I reworked several lines and expanded a thought or two.

When he returned to the suite at the Carlyle that night I was waiting for him. He had attended a reception for women's organizations of Brooklyn, Manhattan, and Staten Island at the Commodore Hotel. Evidently the women of Brooklyn, Manhattan, and Staten Island had mobbed him, for when he stripped off his jacket I saw his shirt was soaked with perspiration.

"I'll have to shut off the air conditioner," he apologized, striding to the window and snapping a switch. "Otherwise I'll have a cold in the morning." He rolled up his sleeves and loosened his tie. "Let's see the speech."

I handed him the four typewritten pages and his eyes raced through them.

"By the way," I said, "Leland Hayward thought you came across poorly on *Meet the Press*. He's offered to advise you on your television technique."

The candidate leaped at the idea. "Terrific. Will you make sure he'll be at the studio tomorrow morning?"

I said I had already asked him and that he had promised to come.

"Call him again and make sure he'll be there," said Kennedy.

It was now past one o'clock in the morning and I decided not to wake Hayward to exact a further assurance.

When I arrived at the Videotape Center the next morning, Leland Hayward had already arrived and was chatting amiably with the agency men. Hayward had been fighting a persistent cold the past two weeks and I reflected that few things could have gotten him out of his bed at this hour on a gray, nasty morning.

No sooner had I walked in the door than one of the admen grabbed me. "This speech is too *short*. I timed it at four minutes," he said.

"That can't be. I timed it in the same cadence the candidate uses and it came out just right." I began reading it with the Kennedy inflection that I often found creeping into my own speech.

"No no no, he won't read it that slowly," said the adman. "I think you'd better add a minute's worth of copy."

I had yielded to the argument and begun scribbling another page of oratory when the candidate and his wife walked into the studio.

"This speech is too long," said Kennedy. "We'll have to make some cuts."

"I'd like you to meet Leland Hayward," I said.

The two shook hands warmly.

"I really appreciate your coming," said Kennedy. "What do you think of the speech?"

"Fine, just fine," said Hayward in the same tone he often used to assure a balky actor that a scene was all right. I half expected him to add, "It will play, it will play."

Hayward suggested that the candidate run through the speech once from the Teleprompter, an instrument Kennedy had never used before. He did so and his reading sounded wooden and uninspired.

"This time, don't *read* it, Bobby," said Hayward. "I've never seen an actor who could use that damn thing. The trick with a Teleprompter is to use it for a *guide.*"

The next run-through sounded more effective.

"That's very good," said Ethel. "Don't you think so, Mr. Hayward?"

"Much better," said Hayward equably. "But I think he can do it even better. Let's try it once more."

The candidate ran through the speech again, this time with Leland Hayward stopping him as he went along, suggesting fine touches of performance. "Bobby, when you say, 'President Kennedy said the torch has been passed,' try to give it more *passion.* Make this sound *important.*"

I cringed but the candidate seemed to take no offense.

"I think we're ready to tape now," said Hayward. "All right, let's film this one."

The agency men exchanged signals, the studio grew quiet, the tiny red light blinked on, and the candidate began.

"I would like to talk to you today about a matter that concerns us all—" and the studio door burst open.

"Hello again," said Shelley Winters. "If there's anything I can do to help—" she began, and again, sensing that this was not the ideal time for volunteering, ducked out again.

"All right, quiet on the set," said the cameraman. "Take two."

The candidate began again. It was a moving few minutes. The speech was a synopsis of many of the things Robert Kennedy had been saying up and down the state —a concise statement of conviction and intention.

I would like [he began] to talk to you today about a matter that concerns us all—the future of our children, the future of our state, the future of our nation.

We live in challenging times. It is the best of times and the worst of times. It is a time of great challenge and tremendous danger.

But it is also a time of great possibility.

It is said that each generation builds a road for the next. I believe each of us has a responsibility to his fellow citizens.

I believe each of us has an obligation to his community, to his state and to his country.

I believe each of us has a responsibility not to be a bystander to the challenges we face.

And it is on this basis that I campaign for the Senate of the United States.

I have roots in the State of New York. I grew up here, attended school here, held my first job here. I lived here for twenty years—far longer than I lived in any other place.

During the last fourteen years I have served the federal government in Washington. And during the past three and a half years I have worked with President Kennedy, and then with President Johnson, to establish the ideals of the New Frontier.

That struggle involved problems directly affecting the people of New York.

The problem of survival.

The problem of avoiding a nuclear holocaust.

The problems of having the young of other nations look to us for leadership instead of to the Soviet Union or Red China.

The internal problems of crime and narcotics and juvenile delinquency.

The struggle for civil rights and civil liberties.

The hopes of our young and the needs of our elderly.

We live in an age of change and challenge. And New York reflects them all. New York is the richest state in the richest nation on earth. Yet New York is also a home to poverty and despair—to neglect and injustice.

I don't think that's satisfactory.

My philosophy differs from my opponent's. And so does my concept of the role a Senator should play.

When I was Attorney General, we believed that public service demanded more of a man that that he wait for problems to reach his desk.

We tried to seek out problems—to lead the fight—to find new ways to do the job. I believe the same applies to a United States Senator.

It has been said that I see New York as a stepping stone to power. The truth is somewhat different. I want New York to be a stepping stone to an ideal.

I believe New York can make a difference.

And I believe a Senator from New York can make a difference.

President Kennedy said in 1961 that "the torch has been passed." The torch was an idea—a hope that

America could solve her problems—that our people could realize their dreams—that no difficulty was so great it could not be solved by the patient work of men who loved their country.

And so in the short time remaining in this campaign, I ask for your help.

And in return I pledge you my energy, and whatever talents I possess. I pledge you my future.

≈≈

CHAPTER 14

The President

In an interview with Robert Kennedy two months before the campaign began, a *New York Times* man had noted a copy of one of my photo-caption books on the Attorney General's desk. The cover photo showed an intense Bob Kennedy whispering into the ear of a seemingly mesmerized Lyndon Johnson. "When you open your eyes," went the caption, "you will do exactly as I say——"

My first day at the Carlyle, Robert Kennedy wanted to know how my little book was selling.

"It's doing fine," I said.

He smiled ruefully. "The cover of Mr. Johnson and me certainly helped our relationship."

Whatever the relationship between the President and the Attorney General, in early August Johnson declared Kennedy—and all his other Cabinet members—ineligible for the Vice-Presidency. Most observers saw this as a transparent device to eliminate Mr. Kennedy without offending Kennedy's supporters by singling him out for repudiation.

Addressing a school for Congressional candidates the

following day, the Attorney General had said wryly, "I must confess I stand in awe of you. You are not members of the Cabinet . . . therefore you are eligible for Vice-President. I've decided to send a little note to Cabinet members in general, saying, 'I'm sorry I took so many nice fellows over the side with me.' "

A few days later the President had invited Kennedy to his office for a friendly chat.

"What did you talk about?" a reporter wanted to know.

"We talked about the campaign for about an hour," said Kennedy. "And then we talked about how bad it was to be Vice-President." Kennedy paused. "He did most of the talking."

As the campaign ground along, one heard it said that President Johnson's elimination of Kennedy for the Vice-Presidency was evidence that the President wanted a Keating victory. Others observed that there was little in Kennedy's standard stump speech that praised Johnson, and read this as further evidence of a coolness between the two.

Early in the campaign Kennedy's advisors saw little merit in emphasizing a close identification between Lyndon Johnson and Robert Kennedy.

"Our slogan," said Fred Papert, "is 'Let's Put Bob Kennedy to Work for New York.' "

"I don't like it," Debs Myers had said. "It should be something like 'Back LBJ with RFK.' "

But Myers had been outvoted.

Then the difficult days of early October had arrived, bringing a sharp diminution of Kennedy's lead.

On October 12 Hubert Horatio Humphrey came to New York.

"There is a team—" said the Vice-Presidential candidate to a tumultuous throng in White Plains. "There is a team that needs your support and has *earned* your support. It is the team of Johnson, Humphrey, and Kennedy."

At that rally and thereafter a new campaign poster blossomed. Its slogan: "Join the Johnson-Humphrey-Kennedy Team."

Being a gentleman to his toes, Debs Myers refused to say, "I told you so."

On October 14 Lyndon Johnson came to town.

It had been quite a week. Khrushchev was out, Brezhnev and Kosygin were in, the Red Chinese bomb was up, the stock market was down, Harold Wilson was in, and Walter Jenkins was out. But the volcanic events did not prevent the President from conducting a whirlwind tour of Buffalo, Rochester, and Brooklyn with Bob Kennedy and lavishing high praise on him at every stop.

The final entry on the Kennedy schedule read: "Balance of the afternoon and evening will be spent with the President at his public appearances, ending with an appearance at the Alfred E. Smith Dinner, Waldorf-Astoria Hotel, Grand Ballroom."

As I read that notation, I recalled the Alfred E. Smith Dinner of 1960. The John Kennedy wit had never crackled more sharply.

"Your Eminence, Cardinal Spellman, Mr. Vice-President, Governor Rockefeller, Mayor Wagner, distinguished guests, ladies and gentlemen, fellow voters," he had begun.

"Cardinal Spellman is the only man so widely respected in American politics that he could bring together, amicably, at the same banquet table, for the first time in this campaign, two political leaders who are increasingly apprehensive about the November election, who have long eyed each other suspiciously, and who have disagreed so strongly, both publicly and privately—Vice-President Nixon and Governor Rockefeller.

"Mr. Nixon, like the rest of us, has had his troubles in this campaign. At one point even the *Wall Street Journal* was criticizing his tactics. That is like the *Osservatore Romano* criticizing the Pope.

"But I think the worst news for the Republicans this week was that Casey Stengel has been fired. It must show that perhaps experience does not count.

"On this matter of experience, I had announced earlier this year that if successful I would not consider campaign contributions as a substitute for experience in appointing ambassadors. Ever since I made that statement I have not received one single cent from my father.

"One of the inspiring notes that was struck in the last debate was struck by the Vice-President in his very moving warning to the children of the nation and the candidates against the use of profanity by Presidents and ex-Presidents when they are on the stump. And I know after fourteen years in Congress with the Vice-President that he was very sincere in his views about the use of profanity. But I am told that a prominent Republican said to him yesterday, 'Mr. Vice-President, that was a damn fine speech.' And the Vice-President said, 'I appreciate the compliment but not the language.' And the Republican went on, 'Yes, sir, I liked it so much that I contributed a thousand dollars to your campaign.' And Mr. Nixon replied, 'The hell you say.' "

With this heady tradition, many were anxious to hear Robert Kennedy's speech at the Alfred E. Smith Dinner in 1964. But they were to be disappointed. The President was invited to speak but the young candidate was not.

That same day, October 14, 1964, brought Robert Kennedy praise from yet another Democratic President, Harry S Truman.

In a letter to the candidate, Truman underlined the importance to a President of having a Senator of his own party speaking for a key state such as New York.

"Senator Wagner was a strong right arm to President Roosevelt, and Senator Lehman was always at my side," wrote Truman. "President Johnson will need the same kind of cooperation from New York."

The press reported the testimonial and duly observed that here was one more example of the new strategy— an all-out attempt to unite the Kennedy candidacy with that of the national ticket.

October 14 produced one other noteworthy endorsement for Robert Kennedy. The intellectual vote.

Bill vandenHeuvel had invited the high priests of salon society and the arts to his high-ceilinged apartment on Central Park West. They came to hear twin testimonials to the candidate's liberality by Arthur Schlesinger, Jr., and John Kenneth Galbraith. It was hoped that the distinguished guests would, in turn, give their own parties and so extend the proselytizing chain.

There were enough celebrities present to serve an addictive name-dropper for months. Leonard Bernstein, Gloria Vanderbilt, Jason Robards, Jr., John Gunther, Jules Feiffer, Adolph Green, Lauren Bacall, Paddy Chayefsky, Abe Burrows, Lillian Hellman, and Jacqueline Kennedy.

Arthur Schlesinger was sitting on a window sill.

"How many votes *are* there in the intellectual bloc?" someone asked him.

"I know it's negligible in numbers. But they do influence the atmosphere of a campaign. Many of the people in this room have the conventional liberal doubts about Bobby."

"Do you think this intellectual opposition can be silenced?"

"I hope so," said Schlesinger.

There was a touch of *déjà vu* about the affair. In 1960 Schlesinger and Galbraith had appeared as character witnesses for another Kennedy who stood accused of being unprincipled and hungry for power. And in 1960 Schlesinger and Galbraith were right.

But now it was 1964. And as I listened to Kenneth Galbraith arguing the liberal credentials of Robert Kennedy to this group of noted artists and intellectuals, it seemed to me incredible and sad that we must go through it all again.

CHAPTER 15

ᕱᕱ

The "Jewish Vote"

Flying home from Buffalo one day in mid-September, Robert Kennedy had confided to Homer Bigart of the *New York Times* that he was worried about "the Jewish vote." Strategically it may have been poor judgment to use such an expression—and even worse, not to declare the conversation off the record. But factually, Kennedy's assessment was painfully accurate. A statewide poll conducted a few weeks earlier among one thousand Jewish New Yorkers showed the slimmest of margins for Kennedy. But even this modest superiority provided no solace to the candidate's aides.

"The poll showed more men than women favoring Bob," said Ed Guthman. "It should be the other way around."

Political leaders in heavily Jewish neighborhoods came to the Carlyle, bearing gloomy prophecies of heavy defections. Four years before Jewish voters had supported John Kennedy overwhelmingly, but no one expected Robert Kennedy to do anywhere near as well.

In his race for Kenneth Keating's Senate seat, Kennedy was—as who isn't—as much the slave of his past as he was its beneficiary. And now some of his acts and associations were denying him the regard of some religious and racial groups whose support might decide the election.

The attitude of Jews toward Robert Kennedy was ambivalent. He looked and sounded enough like his brother to send an eerie feeling through the crowds at Grossinger's and the Concord. When he rode through a Brooklyn street, people would stop as though transfixed by an apparition.

But the coin had another side.

The antagonism between liberal Jews and Irish bosses in the City of New York had a long history. And it was the Irish bosses who were the most energetic promoters in bringing Robert Francis Kennedy into the New York race.

Kennedy had yet another problem with the Jewish people. He must somehow deal with the charge that he was an outsider trying to depose an anti-Goldwater legislator, and that he was a ruthless young man who got what he wanted whoever suffered in the process.

Kennedy's efforts in support of the Civil Rights Bill, his opposition to the bombing of Cuba during the 1962 missile crisis, his little-publicized efforts in support of Washington youth, somehow failed to remove the damning reputation for ambition and arrogance.

So Kennedy did what he could to counteract the Jewish exodus from Democratic ranks. He asked his brother Ted, who was recuperating from his back injuries, to phone Hubert Humphrey and urge him to try to do something during his upcoming visit to Manhattan. And Humphrey, who is a great favorite among New York's

Jewish leaders, promptly urged David Dubinsky to dedicate himself to a solution of "the Jewish problem." So, at a Liberal Party banquet, the Vice-Presidential nominee placed Robert Kennedy in the tradition of Franklin Roosevelt and Herbert Lehman.

Kennedy himself made sure his schedule took him often into the heavily Jewish areas of the city. He wound up one hectic day with a visit to four rabbis. And his chosen traveling companion on most of these excursions was a man whose name and deeds were popular among people of the Jewish faith: Franklin D. Roosevelt, Jr.

Wherever Robert Kennedy ventured in the Jewish neighborhoods of New York City, people responded passionately to the boyish grin, the querulous voice, the agile form. There was always the excited physical rush of the crowd to touch him. But in the pressing throng, the careful observer could always see a great many people who wore a curious combination of Johnson and Keating buttons. And one could only wonder . . .

So it was that as the campaign reached its mid-point, both the Keating and Kennedy camps assessed that "the Jewish vote" was the key to victory.

Keating's asssessment was unarguable. There were 3.2 million enrolled Democrats in New York State and 2.8 million Republicans. Keating must bite into Democratic ranks to retain his seat. The Jewish vote seemed the most logical target because of its size—there were 1.8 million Jewish adults in the State of New York.

According to most professional appraisals, Keating's courtship of New York Jewry was going well. The Senator was extremely popular with the large liberal Jewish population, and indeed he deserved to be. One rabbi observed, "Mr. Keating goes around with a skullcap in his pocket, and every time you put three Jews together, he stands up and makes a speech."

Outward appearances were deceiving. In Jewish areas Kennedy attracted crowds whose hysteria and dimensions beggared those of a Presidential campaign. Keating's crowds were invariably small and sober. Yet the polls irrefutably revealed that New York City's metropolitan Jewish bloc—comprising over a million voters—were going Republican.

This was made evident during Keating's walking tours of the city. For instance, on a stroll through a Jewish section of Greenwich Village, the Senator was stopped by an elderly man who said, "Mr. Keating, I have *never* voted Republican—but I will vote for *you.*"

A middle-aged Jewish housewife in Queens remarked, "At first I thought I'd vote for Kennedy, but now I don't know. You just don't throw out a good man because somebody wants to move in. Tell me—what's Keating done *wrong?*"

Keating's braintrusters were fond of observing that his pro-Israel record and his attendance at civic meetings and bar mitzvahs were paying off. Yet surveys did not really bear this out, for the Jewish defections were not merely pro-Keating. They were also anti-Kennedy.

Many voters, it appeared, were hardly aware of the Senator's existence.

A strong body of opinion—including both sociologists and politicians—contended there was no such thing as "the Jewish vote." Yet knowledgeable pollsters seemed ready to demonstrate that a significant number of Jewish voters *could* be enticed away from their party by an appeal to "certain group tendencies."

In 1962, for example, in a New York Senatorial contest between Democrat James Donovan and Republican Jack Javits, the latter won the votes of 60 percent of the Jewish voters, despite the fact that Republican candidates usually draw only 30 percent of their votes.

But this year the Kennedy-Keating race was forcing a cruel choice on the Jewish voter. Both the contestants had records one would characterize as "liberal." Many Jews would have liked to vote for Kennedy because of their affection for his brother and the appeal of the Kennedy image. But their consciences troubled them and kept them from turning their backs on a man whose record seemed impeccable and who had given unstinting support to Israel.

"Many members of my congregation," said a Brooklyn rabbi, "are struggling with their conscience. They're just sitting on the fence waiting for some issue to develop to see which way they will go."

Senator Kenneth Keating obliged them . . .

On September 20 Senator Keating charged that a firm fronting for Nazis would benefit from Robert Kennedy's settlement, while Attorney General, of the General Aniline and Film Corporation case.

The issue was a sleeper.

One Sunday morning it was tossed into the battle and within twenty-four hours both candidates were hammering away at it with increasing bitterness and many observers were predicting that the turning point of the campaign had been reached.

Keating dropped his bombshell in a speech before the International Chemical Union in Newark, and the charge promptly set afire what had previously been a virtually issueless campaign.

Keating charged that Kennedy had agreed to a settlement that turned over more than $60,000,000 of the assets of GAF to Interhandel. Keating insisted that Interhandel, a Swiss firm, was actually a front, and that much of the money would end up in the hands of I. G. Farben, the giant German chemical firm from which GAF was seized when America entered the war against Nazi Germany.

The day the allegations exploded in the press, a meeting was called at the candidate's Glen Cove home.

I drove out to the white clapboard house, parked in the pebbled roadway, walked between the stone statuettes of the black greyhound dogs standing guard at the entrance, and joined the group seated beside the large, curving swimming pool.

Burke Marshall, head of the Justice Department's Civil Rights Division, was there. So was Arthur Schlesinger, and Richard Neustadt, the political science professor and author of *Presidential Power*, the book that John Kennedy had found so instructive during his early months in the White House. And the ubiquitous Ed Guthman was there, looking furious with himself.

"I was ready for something like this," he said ruefully. "I expected them to spring this General Aniline thing—but that Nazi angle caught me off guard."

When the story of the Keating charge had broken the night before, Guthman had issued an immediate reply for the candidate, denying the charge and pointing out that the Department of Justice had assured that none of the GAF money would go to former Nazis. The statement further noted that the GAF case could have been expected to drag on in the courts for a decade, and added, "As a result of the settlement, more than $100,000,000 was made available to pay war claims of American citizens who suffered at Nazi hands."

There was a good deal more the statement *could* have said.

For example, it could have observed that Kenneth Keating himself had introduced the Senate bill which made the sale possible. And that he was kept advised of the proceedings at the time and gave every indication that he approved.

"We can issue the additional statement today," said Kennedy. There was no rancor in his manner, just a quiet toughness, an air of rueful sincerity—and perhaps a touch of disappointment.

"Now what else can we do to turn this around?"

The Kennedy camp approached every problem with the view that it could somehow be "turned around" and used to their advantage.

"The State Department requested that you make this settlement, didn't they?" asked Schlesinger. "Wouldn't Dean Rusk be willing to make a statement?"

"I don't think that would be helpful," said Kennedy. "Perhaps a statement from Nick would do some good." Nicholas Katzenbach was the Acting Attorney General, appointed by President Johnson after Kennedy's resignation.

"This Keating charge may backfire," said Guthman reflectively. "It's so transparently an appeal for Jewish votes that a lot of people are going to be repelled by it."

"There's another thing," observed Richard Neustadt, and in a dozen words articulated the most far-reaching significance of the attack. "It certainly gives you the justification for attacking *him* for a change."

The next day, at a press conference in the living room of his Carlyle suite, Kennedy did just that. He hit back and he hit back hard, in his strongest personal assault of the campaign.

"In all my experience in political campaigning," said the candidate, tapping sharply on a table for emphasis, "I have never heard of a charge as low as this one. I really expected more from Mr. Keating. I lost a brother and a brother-in-law to the Nazis. I'm not making any deals with Nazis."

On the table beside him was a framed cover from a recent *Life* magazine in which his brother John's two children and four of his own were crawling over the broadly grinning candidate. But he was not grinning now. He seemed older than his *Life* photo. His face was drawn around the mouth. There was a smudge of gray above the ears, and one suspected that the day might not be too far off when people might even stop calling him Bobby.

Judy Michaelson of the *New York Post*, a newspaper with a large Jewish readership, asked the candidate to

comment on Keating's motive in launching his charge
about a "Nazi deal."

"You ask him that," snapped Kennedy.

Then as the rhetorical ball continued to hang in the
air, Kennedy swung again. "In New York, with its heavy
Jewish population, there are so many who have suffered
so much from the Nazis—it can't help but have an
effect."

Terry Smith of the *Tribune* asked if Kennedy thought
Keating was sincere when he said he didn't know if his
charge would affect Jewish votes.

"No," said Kennedy.

A reporter reminded the candidate that Mr. Keating
had backtracked from his initial charge by saying he
"had no proof of improper acts" on Kennedy's part, only
that he thought the Attorney General had acted "im-
providently."

"Yes, now he waters it down and says he didn't mean
it. But it still comes as a shock and I received it with a
good deal of bitterness. And I still believe it's going to
have an adverse effect on me. People only remember the
headline above the original story—not the denial. You
never catch up with this sort of thing."

The reporters left to file their stories, and Kennedy's
aides continued to pick at the subject like a bad tooth.

"I'm not so sure that Keating hasn't tossed a boomer-
ang," said Debs Myers. "Until now he's had the image
of being a liberal, decent fellow. Then he hits you with a
scurrilous charge like this— Well, it just might backfire."

Bernie Ruggieri nodded. "The first rule in these
things," he said, "is to be able to make them *stick*. Keating can't do that."

"If there's anything people are sensitive to," put in Guthman, "it's character assassination. I think he may have handed us a lemon and we just might make ourselves some lemonade."

The lemonade tasted fine.

The *New York Times* called the charge "a fake issue," and said that Mr. Keating was obviously playing on what he hoped to be voter ignorance. "Attorney General Kennedy," editorialized the *Times*, "did not make 'a deal with Nazis.' He settled an incredibly complicated lawsuit."

The *Post* said that Keating "dishonored himself" with his charge and called the accusation "outrageous." "Desperation," observed the *Post*, "seems to have become a prevailing mood of Republican politics. It is a familiar last resort."

But again it was the graceful, heavily ironic prose of the *World-Telegram*'s Murray Kempton that expressed it best:

> Keating, for three weeks now has run in this city with an absolute contempt for the intelligence and balance of its citizens. He has operated on the theory that you may not have to be Jewish to eat Levy's bread in New York, but you have to be Jewish and Jewish in caricature to vote there. He has promised to take Israel into NATO, to go to Moscow to tell Khrushchev to stop abusing the Jews . . . and to serve an ultimatum on Nasser.
>
> Both candidates have campaigned on the insulting premise that Jewish voters care about nothing but "Jewish" issues; but where Kennedy has been

unfortunate on occasion, Keating has been incessantly distressing. . . .

And now I promise to say no more, not even to notice that the latest attack on Robert Kennedy's "naked, brazen, power grab" has come from Thomas E. Dewey, whose gentle spiritual direction of their party is remembered by all the Republicans who served him if only because the calluses are still on their knees and his shoe polish indelibly on their noses.

But just how indelibly Senator Keating's assertions had been imprinted on the minds of Jewish New Yorkers —as a meaningful issue or as an outrageous smear— would not be known until the third of November.

CHAPTER 16

◙

The Negro

8:30 P.M.—*Nagel and Seamon Avenues—Rally.*
9:15 P.M.—*Arrive 145th St. and Broadway—Rally.*
10:00 P.M.—*Arrive 127th St. and 7th Ave.—Rally.*

Robert Kennedy was in Harlem.

He stood in the pale convertible with his left hand in his jacket pocket and the wind blowing through his uncombed hair, and his right hand described the little half-wave. And the crowds were tumultuous.

On the press bus I was seated beside Burke Marshall, Robert Kennedy's modest but immensely effective head of the Justice Department's Civil Rights Division. We looked out the tinted windows at the bleak panorama of tenements, the antiquated, overcrowded homes, and then we turned to the laughing faces of the young people racing along after the candidate's car. There was only one word to explain their joy or their intensity of feeling. It was hope.

The press bus came to a halt. We had reached the last stop on our schedule, scarcely two hours late.

Carol Ash came down the aisle. "Come on," she said. "Let's get a little closer."

Carol and I left the bus and moved through the throng on the darkened street and slowly worked our way to the auto behind Kennedy's car. We climbed on the trunk for a better view of the candidate, who had fought his way through the dense crowd and finally gained the top of a nearby sound truck. He was talking about the problem of drop-outs and looking intently into the faces of the youngsters around him. "I want you all to promise me you're not going to drop out of school. You're going to *need* your education."

He talked about solutions to the drop-out problem— loans for the needy, remedial training for backward students, part-time employment for others.

"The civil rights law," shouted Kennedy over the midnight din, "was just a step. But this trip is a thousand miles. So when I look back over the last three and a half years, I feel we've turned a corner. But we have unfinished business. We've just begun. We have great things to do."

And then came the familiar terminal words, "So I come to Harlem and I ask for your help—"

"I'm going back to the bus," said Carol Ash a little uncertainly, as the candidate climbed down from the sound truck and headed for his car, followed by the surging crowd.

"I'll see you there," I said.

Then suddenly, for some unexplained reason, the candidate pointed and his aides headed him toward the automobile on which *I* was perched. The storm of bodies, with Robert Kennedy as its eye, beat in upon the car. Escape was impossible.

Kennedy mounted the rear deck of the convertible, his ankles and calves grasped firmly by Dean Markham and Jim King, who were kneeling on the back seat. The thousands of shouting, near-hysterical people came charging at the car from all directions. The car began to move and the crowd rushed after it. Five struggling, perspiring policemen, cursing noiselessly, ran after the car, trying vainly to keep the mob behind them. Kennedy made their task the more difficult—and my position at his feet the more precarious—by reaching out his hands to the crowd.

Trapped on the rear deck of the slowly moving auto, with the mob of impassioned citizens rushing headlong toward us, the line of policemen seemed to stand between us and annihilation, and annihilation was winning. A dozen times the line gave way and teen-agers rushed through, clambering up onto the car before policemen grabbed them and hurled them back into the crowd.

The thought raced through my mind that one injured woman or one injured youth—since all the police officers were white—might trigger a small riot.

The car seemed to be outdistancing its ardent pursuers when suddenly one of the tires went flat. Perhaps it was the excessive weight of its captive passengers. Perhaps an act of malice or sabotage. But whatever the cause, the crowd was on us again. But the driver saw the danger of stopping and continued to clank along on three tires and a metal rim.

And then a *second* tire went flat.

The car rumbled doggedly along like a disabled tank, but after less than half a block it finally ground to a halt.

The crowd was now clearly the master. In a stationary position, it was impossible for the small band of policemen to keep the crowds from inundating the car and the candidate. Kennedy's aides quickly surrounded him and forced their way to a nearby police car whose tires were all intact, and he made good his escape.

Peter Maas, the magazine writer with whom I had been stranded on the car's rear deck, looked around for signs of the motorcade. There were none. The press bus and the other cars were by now on some remote avenue in midtown.

There was a battle-zone quality to the whole affair. After a few minutes a car bearing the insignia of CBS News approached us. We flagged it down and asked for transportation back to a rear echelon. The driver, happily, agreed.

As we drove south, we exchanged battle experiences.

"I nearly got killed," said the CBS man.

"I had nothing to hold onto," I said.

"I was holding onto Kennedy's thigh," said Peter Maas.

"Name-dropper," I said.

Even before Robert Kennedy's volcanic reception in Harlem, it had been foreseen that he would receive most of New York's sizable Negro vote. But there was speculation as to whether it would be an enthusiastic endorsement. The uncertainty stemmed from what many saw as a reluctance to take an outspoken position in the campaign on certain issues of Negro rights.

The major civil rights groups had endorsed neither Kennedy nor Keating. Some claimed this was because both candidates had good records on civil rights. Others said that all the resources of the rights organizations were being mustered to defeat Barry Goldwater.

But those most familiar with the civil rights groups insisted there was no endorsement for quite another reason—the leaders wanted Keating while the rank-and-file members wanted Kennedy.

They remembered him as the man who got James Meredith into the University of Mississippi. They remembered him as the one who sent Nick Katzenbach to face down Governor George Wallace in a schoolhouse door and get Vivian Malone and Jimmy Hood into the University of Alabama. They remembered, and they wanted him in the Senate.

Even those Negroes who strongly supported Kenneth Keating hesitated to attack Bob Kennedy. As one put it, "Attacking Bobby is almost like attacking his brother. Nobody's going to do *that*."

A notable exception to this rule of reticence was former ballplayer Jackie Robinson. Writing in the influential Negro newspaper, the *Amsterdam News*, he said, "It cannot truthfully be said that Robert Kennedy's record as Attorney General is spotless or perfectly consistent in defense of the rights of the Negro people. Let us not forget the several occasions when the civil rights struggle was at its height in crucial areas and Robert Kennedy seriously undercut the position of the civil rights leadership by calling for the Negro to 'go slow.' And the almost unbroken FBI record of coming up with blanks in solving civil rights murders and church bombings did not measurably improve under Bob Kennedy."

Another columnist with a commitment to Negro rights held a different view. Said Harry Golden, publisher of the *Carolina Israelite*, "Robert Kennedy delivered the death blow to the Southern caste system. And for the first time in a hundred years Southern Negroes believed a white man. Robert Kennedy had asked them to sign complaints and affidavits and they complied by the thousands. They had never signed their names to a complaint before. This was the first time. They believed Robert Kennedy. With these complaints as evidence, Robert Kennedy set off to destroy the inequities of a segregated caste system in sixty-four cases in three years based on the Civil Rights Act of 1957. The previous Eisenhower Administration, which had this law for the same length of time, had initiated *six* cases, and two of those on the Administration's last day."

But Kenneth Keating had other cards to play. One of these was dealt from the hand of his Republican colleague, Jack Javits, who lashed out at Kennedy, saying that as Attorney General he had approved the appointment of federal judges who believed in segregation.

Kennedy responded by pointing out that prospective judges were recommended by the American Bar Association and must be approved by the Senate Judiciary Committee on which Kenneth Keating was a member. "Not only did Senator Keating not *object* to the appointments," said Kennedy, "he didn't even show up for the *hearings*."

But Jack Javits had a devoted following in New York

City and his attacks were telling. When Bill vanden-Heuvel heard the Javits assault he said, "I met Jack Javits in Europe this summer and he advised me to urge Bob not to run in New York. He said, 'Tell him if he does we'll clobber him.' "

But it was not an easy matter to fault Robert Kennedy's work in the field of civil rights. For it was incontestable that racial equality had advanced further and faster during his tenure than under any previous Attorney General. The Kennedy formula was to use force only when all means of persuasion failed. But when such an alternative was pressed on him, he never gave an inch.

In a personal meeting with Wallace of Alabama and in numerous phone conversations with Barnett of Mississippi, Kennedy had tried to persuade them to comply peacefully with federal desegregation orders. And in the absence of screaming headlines, many failed to notice that in the fall of 1964—for the first time—school desegregation in the South moved ahead virtually without incident.

It was also irrefutably true that Robert Kennedy's Justice Department wrote the strongest civil rights bill in American history and that he helped nurse it through an often unwilling Congress.

Later he convened a series of meetings with Southern businessmen to explain the torchy public accommodations clause and underline the Justice Department's commitment to enforce it.

As the *Amsterdam News* editorialized—a few days after their columnist Jackie Robinson had taken a contrary position: "No Attorney General in the history of

America has more aggressively placed the weight of that office behind the interest of fair play and welfare of minority groups. He was a great Attorney General and we believe he will make a great Senator. We therefore urge his election."

Mounting registration drives among minority groups is an old Kennedy weapon. It helped Jack Kennedy build heavy pluralities in the large cities in 1960. And Bob Kennedy was using it to try to defeat Kenneth Keating in 1964.

What had started out as an important factor in Bob Kennedy's election plans—the votes of new registrants—suddenly became a crucial one when his lead began to shrink in early October.

"These Negro votes were supposed to be the frosting," said Steve Smith. "But they're turning into the *cake*."

The Democrats had taken on the major burden of enrolling new voters. It was a socially desirable undertaking—with frankly self-serving ends. A Republican official explained, with refreshing candor, his party's indifference to lengthening the rolls. "With Harlem voting ten to one against us," he said, "don't you think we'd be a little silly to register more voters?"

So in early October the Kennedy organization began a massive telephone operation. Their goal was to get a hundred thousand unregistered people to the five thousand registration desks spotted throughout the city. The Kennedys always aim high.

Full-page newspaper ads were run showing a typical voter-literacy test, to convince Negroes it was not as difficult as they might suppose.

One galling aspect of the registration drive was the fact that in many districts controlled by the old-line party bosses, the Democratic leaders were sitting on their hands. The local chieftains saw in a flood of new voters a threat to their district control. And their inertia threatened to deprive Kennedy of tens of thousands of votes that could mean the difference between defeat and victory.

So Kennedy bypassed them. The candidate marshaled his *own* registration drive in Negro areas. He campaigned vigorously at the Harlem rallies, knowing that sentiment there was strongly Democratic and there would be little inclination to ticket-splitting.

Meanwhile hundreds of volunteers were dispatched from labor unions and social welfare groups to swarm over Negro districts in search of unregistered residents. Handbills rained on the area, posters were plastered everywhere, and sound trucks patrolled the streets, blaring their appeals to the unregistered.

Predictably enough, the highest rate of new registration was in Harlem. The lowest rate was in the Bronx, where regular Democratic party leaders were doing virtually nothing to register new voters. Ironically, the districts gripped by registration lethargy were those controlled by Charles A. Buckley, who was one of Robert Kennedy's earliest and staunchest supporters.

Buckley was an albatross that Kennedy refused to abandon despite the most pestiferous prodding of the press. Kennedy had supported Buckley in the spring primary against Jack Bingham, the Democrats' reform candidate.

At a press conference in Rochester the question had erupted for the umpteenth time.

"Mr. Keating said today that you're the candidate of the bosses," said a reporter.

"I have only one boss and she's at home," said the candidate.

"But what about Charley Buckley?" said the reporter.

"Charley Buckley gave us his help in 1960 when my brother needed it," said the candidate. "He was the same man in 1964. If he was good enough to ask for his help when *we* needed it, he was good enough to *get* our help when *he* needed it." Then Kennedy paused and added thoughtfully, "And that's the way it should be between men."

Even though Kennedy's civil rights credentials seemed for the most part unassailable, the block of Negro votes was a sizable one, and so in early October, Keating attacked Kennedy's record.

"Robert Kennedy abandoned his post," charged Kenneth Keating in the advance text of a speech to be delivered at the NAACP state convention in Buffalo. "He abandoned his post at the Department of Justice with the unfinished task before him—the task of putting teeth into the new law and defending it against attack on its constitutionality."

But when Keating rose to speak before the group, for some reason he omitted this vehement attack. "I have not come here to bury Bobby, but to praise him—" he said. Then he cited his own record in behalf of civil rights. "I was the author of the civil rights bill which passed the House in 1956 and 1957—"

Keating was followed at the podium by Charles

Evers, the brother of Medgar Evers, the slain civil rights worker. "Robert Kennedy," he said, "is the one man who cared. If we were fortunate enough to have a man like Mr. Kennedy running even for *dog catcher*, he'd get every vote a Negro would have in Mississippi."

Evers paused. "And one more thing. I wouldn't be alive today if it wasn't for Bob Kennedy."

When the Senator finally descended from the platform he faced a group of reporters who had noticed the striking disparity between his printed and his delivered speech.

"Senator, are you withdrawing the sharper attack on Mr. Kennedy contained in your advance text?"

"I stand by the advance text," said Keating.

At his hotel in Syracuse, Robert Kennedy was given the news as he was changing his clothes before his final stop of the day.

"Isn't that incredible?" he said grimly. "He wouldn't say that in front of the NAACP because they *know* my record. But now up and down the state the headlines will carry the charge that I walked out on the Negro."

The candidate's final stop of the day was to be Syracuse University.

"Where's my speech?" he asked.

Ed Guthman retrieved it from the dresser where it lay in a pile of notes, briefing sheets, and loose change. Kennedy sat down on the bed and began scribbling on the back of the first page.

"Kenneth Keating," he wrote in his cramped handwriting, "is conducting a campaign based on a most cynical exploitation of ethnic groups. First he accused me of making a 'deal' with Nazis. Then of being anti-Italian. Today he has charged that I sold out the Negro.

"These charges have two things in common. First, they are clearly intended to prejudice voters with claims" —he continued on the back of the second sheet—"that are transparently false. And second, they are issued by press release rather than before an audience of the people concerned—because my opponent knows they would be rejected by anyone who knows my record."

Having done this, the candidate sighed ponderously, folded the sheets lengthwise, and shoved them into the pocket of his glen plaid jacket.

"There," said Kennedy with satisfaction.

CHAPTER 17

▶◀

The Empty Chair

"I've been campaigning for four weeks now and the only thing that's come across is that I'm a Beatle," said Robert Kennedy as he paced the living room of his Carlyle suite.

It was early October and over the past few weeks the polls had shown a steep slide away from Kennedy—both private and public polls showed a five percent gain for the incumbent.

Some said that people were disappointed in Kennedy's fuzzy generalities on the stump and his unwillingness to attack Keating directly. Yet whenever Kennedy made a speech on a substantive subject, the newspaper stories would contrive to headline the massive crowds. Some said these very crowds had seduced Kennedy into running as though he were already the incumbent. Some said it was the carpetbagger issue and the gradual evaporation of the initial Kennedy glamour.

But whatever the reason, there was no question that the healthy gap separating the two candidates was inexorably closing.

A meeting had been called in the candidate's suite to discuss what could be done to arrest the trend. There was an atmosphere of sobriety to the group. There was no sign of the antic quality that always lurked just beneath the surface at such a gathering of the Kennedy top brass.

When he finally spoke, Robert Kennedy's eyes were fixed on the beige carpet. "I think we're going to have to debate."

Kennedy's advisers—particularly Steve Smith—had been reluctant to have their man debate the elder Senator. It was not any lack of confidence in his forensic skill. Kennedy had demonstrated a surprising flare for extemporaneous debate, much more so than his opponent. It was felt, however, that the TV debate was traditionally the weapon of the underdog, because the front-runner had everything to lose and nothing to gain.

In Kennedy's case there was another meaningful deterrent. In a face-to-face encounter there was the feeling that Kennedy might appear as a brash young prosecutor in hurling questions and rebutting answers from his mature, white-maned opponent.

A fine example of the hazards of television debate was provided by the confrontation of Pierre Salinger and George Murphy in the California Senatorial race. Salinger had gone into the debate the favorite. He had tossed back knowing answers to all the questions, and observers agreed he had shown Murphy up as inadequately informed. Salinger had won the debates—and delivered countless votes to Murphy, "the good guy."

So all things considered, the Kennedy forces were not hungering for debate if it could be honorably avoided.

And that was the view until this disturbing day in early October.

"I have to do something to stop this trend," said Kennedy. "The Lubbell Poll says I'm already behind. I don't think that's so. But the trend is certainly away from me and we're going to have to do something."

"That Lubell Poll," said Steve Smith, "is going to be a help. It's going to give you something you've never had until now—the look of an underdog."

"At this rate," said Debs Myers, "inside of a week he *will* be an underdog."

"You called it back in August," said Guthman. "You said you'd start with celebrity appeal and be well ahead in early September. Then you'd go down and hit your low point the first week in October."

"The question," said Steve Smith, "is whether we keep going down or do something to bring it back up."

"Is there anyone here who's against me debating?" said Kennedy, and looked about the room.

"I am," said Bernie Ruggieri. "You'll have to attack him, and to whatever extent you're successful, you'll be building his sympathy vote. At least I'm against it *now*. Perhaps next week, if things continue to deteriorate—"

"Next week will be too late," said the candidate. "Next week Keating could reasonably say that his schedule is set for the rest of the campaign. He can't say that today. We have to decide now." He looked around the room. "Anybody else opposed?" No one spoke.

"All right," he said. "We debate."

There was silence throughout the room. It was apparent that Kennedy's advisors did not relish the confrontation.

"I might not need it," said Kennedy, "but if I lost and I hadn't debated, I'd never forgive myself."

"You shouldn't challenge him," said Debs Myers. "That might sound arrogant. You should put it in the form of accepting *his* challenge of a month ago. Remember he was saying then he would be willing to debate the issues."

"What about format?" said Steve Smith.

"Let's stipulate the format of the Kennedy-Nixon debates of 1960," said the candidate.

"There'll be a problem about the equal-time law," observed Ed Guthman.

He referred to a federal law requiring that television time be dispensed equally to minority party candidates. Congress had waived the equal-time requirement for the Kennedy-Nixon debates, but they had taken no such action this year.

"We'll just offer to buy the time. We'll pay for half of it and suggest the Keating organization pay for the other half," said Kennedy.

"When people read the story tomorrow they're going to assume you want to debate because you think you're losing," said Myers.

Kennedy weighed that one for a moment. "Just say that Mr. Keating has accused me of such lofty actions as making a 'deal' with Nazis, selling out the Negroes, and being anti-Italian. Say that I'd like him to make in my presence the charges he makes so freely when we're miles apart. Say *that's* why I want the debates."

"Did somebody get that down?" said Myers.

It was decided that Kennedy would extend the challenge—or accept the Keating challenge—in a speech he was scheduled to deliver that evening before the International Brotherhood of Electrical Workers. It would be issued to the press simultaneously in mimeographed statement form. Debs Myers headed toward the front door. He wore an anguished look.

"Cheer up," said Ed Guthman.

"I'm just concerned that Keating might say something outrageous and get Bob's dander up. In thirty seconds the whole election could go out the window."

Guthman didn't answer him directly. "I remember," he said, "one long night we spent in his office at the Justice Department during the Freedom Rider crisis in 1961. Three thousand Negroes had taken refuge in an Alabama church, and there were mobs of angry whites surrounding it. A hundred U.S. marshals had kept the mob at bay until finally Governor John Paterson sent in state troopers and National Guardsmen. It was almost two A.M. when the Governor suddenly phoned Bob and started berating him. And I remember Bob saying, 'Now, John, don't tell *me* that. That's all right for TV, John. Now come on, John—' "

"You think he'll keep cool," said Myers.

"I think he'll keep cool," said Guthman.

Politics develops the quality of twenty-twenty hindsight. And with such retrospective vision it is easy to observe today that Keating played it all wrong. No sooner did the Lubbell Poll announce that Kennedy had fallen behind, than Kenneth Keating rushed to embrace the finding and claim it as fact. He thus handed Kennedy the one thing he needed desperately—the appealing image of the underdog rather than the unattractive look of the young dynamo overpowering everything in his path.

"If the election were held today, I'd win!" Keating told a Harlem audience of fewer than a hundred people, where a few days before Kennedy had drawn a few thousand.

"Senator Keating has caught up and pulled slightly ahead," said his campaign manager, former Attorney General Herbert Brownell. Yet there was nothing in the meager crowds that greeted the incumbent to support this rosy view.

The verities of the situation were more nearly expressed by a news magazine poll which showed Kennedy still leading with 52 percent of the vote to Keating's 48 percent.

So once again there was to be a debate. The press and public were excited by the idea. There was a touch of drama in a new series of debates featuring another Kennedy—though his adversary would bear little resemblance to Richard M. Nixon.

The press pounced on the challenge and carried it to Senator Keating, who reminded them that he had proposed the debates a month before and concluded that he had "no objections" to Kennedy's ground rules.

It was quite true that in early September, Keating had said, "I would be glad to debate." But he had always stopped short of an explicit challenge. Kenneth Keating was undoubtedly as reluctant to debate as was Kennedy—but for somewhat different reasons.

Though Keating would present a most impressive

Senatorial figure and his opponent might look boyish by contrast, there was the chance that Kennedy might once and for all shatter the illusion of himself as a ruthless, power-hungry young man. And maintaining this image, along with the carpetbagger issue, was about the strongest thing Keating had going for him.

This is where the peril lay for Keating—that Kennedy would present a picture of selfless youth and vigor. And an inevitable reminder of another Kennedy in another debate.

When it was reported that Kenneth B. Keating found Kennedy's proposals for a debate acceptable, many New Yorkers assumed that the first of the two debates would be held the following week. Most people wanted it to be so, and the wish is the father to the thought. A debate would add a spark to a campaign that had bogged down in fuzzy generalities and intemperate accusations. Even on the national scene the rhetoric was no better—one could choose between the syrupy inspiration of the President and the depressing pugnacity of Barry Goldwater.

Like the photographers on the press bus who urged the teen-age bicycle riders to acts of recklessness, the reporters were delighted at the prospects of a debate. Most of them agreed that Nixon had been something of a fool to debate in 1960 and give John Kennedy such a splendid showcase for his idealism and wit. But these same reporters found it hard to say just *who* was the fool in the coming encounter. Both candidates had much to lose in the debates, though each had much to gain.

The seconds for the TV duel had been chosen—campaign manager Herb Brownell for the Senator, City Council President Paul Screvane for the challenger.

And then the stalemate developed.

The Keating people decided they wanted no part of the Kennedy-Nixon format. Instead they proposed two arrangements. In the first debate, the candidates would be in separate studios at different times, and they would be questioned by a group of young people, rather than newsmen.

In the second debate, the candidates would be in the same studio, but each would make a series of alternating speeches in the classical manner of Cicero and Demosthenes.

"Does he call that a debate?" said Kennedy when he heard the proposals. "In one of them we're in separate studios. In the other we're making speeches at one another."

For two weeks the stalemate continued, with Kennedy piling up mileage by disparaging the idea of two candidates in separate studios answering questions from youngsters rather than seasoned journalists. These proposals were so transparently inconsistent with genuine debate that Kennedy was able to use them to good advantage, and the polls started to show an encouraging turn.

And then the issue was thrown away . . .

Press secretary Debs Meyers had taken a call from the *New York Times*, listened, shuddered ponderously, and put his hand over the mouthpiece. "Oh my God," he said simply.

"What's the matter, Debs?" I said.

"The *Times* just learned that Kennedy is scheduled

to appear on a TV program with Keating—in separate studios, at separate times, questioned by young people!"

"How the devil did *that* happen?" I said.

"I don't know. I guess we agreed to it months ago, before this business of a debate arose. But the way the *Times* is preparing to write the story, Kennedy has accepted Keating's separate-studio proposal and this is the debate. We really blew *that* issue."

Myers took his hand from the receiver. "Look," he said patiently to the *Times* man, "we agreed to that program a *month* ago. The candidate *never* viewed it as a debate because it obviously *isn't* a debate. We're going through with it because something is better than *nothing*. But for Senator Keating to consider it a debate is *ludicrous*."

Myers listened a moment. "Yes, you can quote me. An authoritative source close to the candidate!" And he banged down the phone.

"They're out to get us," said Myers dourly.

The debate that was not a debate came and went. Few people considered it a debate, and the clamor continued for a genuine confrontation. Then with two weeks remaining in the campaign, CBS suddenly offered to provide an hour of prime evening time for a television debate. And both sides accepted.

The problem, of course, had never been one of *time*, but of *ground rules*. So once again Brownell and Screvane, the two seconds, revived the negotiations that had broken down the week before. And once again the press headlined the imminence of the hour of truth.

The afternoon of CBS's D-Day arrived and an understanding was still to be reached. There were recriminations and accusations of bad faith on both sides. Brownell swore that Screvane had never presented himself at CBS. Screvane insisted that CBS could not reach Brownell for a discussion of format. And CBS, as befits a responsible network anxious to offend no one, said nothing.

As the afternoon wore on, several things happened in the manner of a chess game. Senator Keating purchased the first half of the hour CBS had set aside. Kennedy sought to purchase the second half and was refused, whereupon he communicated directly with CBS President William Paley in California and got his half-hour.

Keating held a high card and prepared to play it during his thirty minutes. The day before, the Fair Campaign Practices Committee had sent a letter to Kennedy accusing him of misrepresenting his opponent's position on the test-ban treaty. The letter was leaked to the press by a committee employee and it appeared that Keating had found a most damaging issue.

But as the day progressed, the issue evaporated. Several prominent members of the FCPC protested that they had known nothing of the letter and thought it unfair. One member resigned in anger. Additional facts were provided and the committee acknowledged its error and withdrew the letter.

Finding himself deprived of this issue, Kenneth Keating arranged for Jacob Javits to join him on the program. Kennedy arranged for the late-night radio conversationalist, Barry Gray, to appear with him as questioner.

Then Keating announced to the press he would appear on *his* half-hour and debate an empty chair, in the time-honored way of dramatizing an opponent's unwillingness to debate.

And that is where the matter stood at 7:00 P.M. that evening, with Keating scheduled to go on the air "live" at 7:30. At the Carlyle there was an aura of tension and dissatisfaction. Leland Hayward had just returned from CBS after reconnoitering the Keating studio. Barry Gray was scribbling questions to ask the candidate. Ed Guthman was calling Louis Nizer to ask him to make an appearance. A half-dozen other aides were scurrying about preparing exhibits for the Kennedy half-hour. The well-oiled Kennedy machine had a decidedly frantic look. But not the candidate.

Finally we all congregated in one of the smaller bedrooms. Bob Kennedy was sitting on the bed, jacketless, shoeless, his sleeves rolled up, his black necktie loosened.

"I can't let him debate an empty chair," said the candidate evenly.

"But what can you do, Bobby?" said Hayward.

"I'm going down there and sit in that empty chair."

"You mean with no ground rules? You'll just barge in and sit down and start debating?"

Kennedy was silent.

"Perhaps you ought to bring a few newsmen with you and offer to debate in the format of the Kennedy-Nixon debates," said Bill vandenHeuvel.

"What will you do if Keating demands to share *your* half-hour?" said Steve Smith.

"You know, Javits is there with Keating," injected

Barry Gray. "There'll be two elder statesmen against one young challenger."

"What time is it?" said Kennedy.

Someone told him it was 7 :05.

"I think I'd better get going."

Hayward, vandenHeuvel, and I arrived first at the CBS studios on West 57th Street and Tenth Avenue. A bevy of newsmen crowded the sidewalk. We had left the Carlyle separately from the candidate so that he would not arrive with so formidable-looking an entourage.

"Has Kennedy arrived yet?" I asked the newsmen. They shook their heads. We waited on the sidewalk until 7 :20, then asked a CBS page to show us to Studio 45, from which Kennedy would broadcast.

As the minutes ticked by we were growing increasingly apprehensive, when a door opened and Kennedy came striding through it. "Where's Senator Keating's studio?" he demanded.

"Your studio is right this way, sir," said the page.

"I said I wanted Mr. *Keating's* studio. Number 44. Where is it?"

Hayward had been there earlier in the day and now led the way down a long corridor. The corridor ended in a closed door and a CBS official with his back to it.

It was now 7 :29 P.M.—one minute to air time for Senator Kenneth Keating.

"I'm here to debate," said Kennedy.

"I'm sorry, sir, I can't let you in."

The crush of newsmen and cameramen was backed up twenty feet behind Kennedy in the narrow, low-ceilinged corridor. Flash bulbs exploded, movie cameras churned, and reporters pressed in to catch the dialogue.

"Senator Keating said he wanted to debate me. He said he would have an empty chair for me. Well, I'm here and I want to go in."

"I'm sorry," said the CBS official, his face drained of expression. "Mr. Keating has purchased this time and I can't permit you to enter."

"Will you tell him I'm here," said Kennedy.

The man thought a moment, then wheeled and disappeared into the studio. It was now just 7:30. An idea occurred to me, and I retraced my steps back to the control room through which we had passed. As I suspected, it was the control room for Studio 44—the Keating studio. On the multiple screens were various shots of the studio behind the door. There was Senator Keating, in white mane and purple prose. There was Senator Javits looking righteously indignant. And there was the empty chair, with the nameplate of Robert F. Kennedy before it.

The program had just begun and an announcer was saying, "Senator Keating has invited his opponent to debate him tonight, but Mr. Kennedy has not appeared—"

That was what I had expected to hear. I darted out of the control room and down the corridor, elbowing my way through layers of newsmen. The CBS man had reappeared, looking even paler than before, and was insisting that Mr. Kennedy could not enter the studio. I whispered to Kennedy what I had just heard.

"They have just announced on the air that I am not

here," said the candidate. "This is very unfair and I insist on being admitted."

The CBS man stood his ground, and the candidate finally retreated to his own studio to prepare for the following half-hour. Though he was frowning on the outside, there was little doubt he was smiling on the inside. He had been barred from a studio in which his absence was being decried, and the representatives of all the New York papers, as well as the wire services, had seen it happen.

But none of us could have anticipated how Kennedy's gain would be further compounded.

When the Keating half-hour ended, reporters besieged his studio to question him on his unwillingness to admit his opponent. Keating came dashing out the studio door behind a phalanx of aides and rushed headlong down the hallway, followed by a battalion of reporters and photographers. In order to hinder their pursuers and permit their chief to make good his escape, Keating's aides began hurling furniture and props in their path.

It was this moment that Mrs. Robert Kennedy chose to descend a stairway overlooking the scene and found herself observing the frantic aides and elder statesman fleeing in disarray, the charging correspondents, photographers, and film cameramen.

"Is anything wrong?" said Ethel Kennedy in the nicest display of understatement of the campaign.

In Studio 44 the scene was somewhat less frantic. But not much. CBS pages were trying without success to empty the place of newsmen. One of them asked Ed

Guthman for his help in this venture, and recalling his shabby treatment at their hands, he flatly refused. "If the press wants to be here, it's all right with us," he said.

Louis Nizer was gazing about with curiosity and detachment. Barry Gray was poring over his questions. Leland Hayward was adjusting the camera angles to favor Kennedy and not present Barry Gray quite so prominently. "He's not running for anything, is he?" he said.

A few minutes before air time an official insisted that the studio be cleared of all those aides and newsmen who were not participating in the broadcast. A young page said he would show us to a screening room where we could observe the show on a monitor. We started out, trudging through what seemed a mile of CBS studio corridors.

"Where the hell is this screening room?" said a reporter, looking nervously at his watch. "At NBC?"

We finally reached Screening Room B and the page left us. The group of newsmen sat crouched before the TV monitor, their pads and pencils at the ready. Zero hour—8:00 P.M.—came and went, and still the screen remained blank. Someone dove for a telephone at the back of the room and announced that the line was dead.

It was a conspiracy! It had to be a conspiracy!

We raced out of the room, cursing the anonymous page and searching for Screening Room A. After a few feverish minutes we found it, and there on the monitor was the candidate being questioned by Barry Gray, looking as composed as though this broadcast had been rehearsed for weeks . . .

After the program Kennedy and his wife made a triumphal exit from the studio. The reporters, who had suffered the indignity of a Keystone Cops pursuit down this same corridor a half-hour before, now had a willing candidate.

The final question related to the headlong flight of his opponent. "Mr. Kennedy, have you any explanation for Mr. Keating's hasty exit?"

"That's *your* problem," said the candidate, and walked toward the elevator.

As the Kennedys waited, still surrounded by the press, a CBS official tried to make belated amends. Television is sensitive to the opinion of powerful men.

"I'm terribly sorry about these difficulties, Mr. Kennedy," he said. "We just try to do our best—"

"That's all right," said Kennedy with a wicked grin. "We'll try to make up for your shortcomings."

"But it won't be easy," said Ethel to a roar of laughter, and they marched onto the elevator.

CHAPTER 18

The Great Debate

"A funny thing happened to me on the way to the studio—" said Robert Kennedy.

The non-debate at the studios of CBS, coming as it did in the crucial closing days of the campaign, gave Kennedy an opportunity for a bit of vote-making raillery.

"Senator Keating really kicked that empty chair all over the studio. No question about it. He beat that chair. And there I was, outside the studio door with three of his guards."

Kennedy sensed that the non-debate had nipped a closing surge for Kenneth Keating. And polls seemed to support this view. After the dramatic events at Studio 44, a pro-Kennedy trend made itself felt—both in New York City and upstate—and the momentum seemed to be growing.

Reporters who had run the Keating obstacle course as his aides tossed chairs and potted plants in their path, had gone out of their way not to favor either candidate in their printed stories, preferring to call the evening a draw. But the events spoke loudly enough not to require any editorial comment. The picture of Kennedy before a sealed door and that of Keating scurrying down a corridor carried their own inevitable implications.

Observers saw another reason for the Kennedy gains in these closing days of the campaign. Senator Keating, they said, was not providing his supporters with any positive arguments in his own behalf. His emphasis continued to be on denigrating his opponent's qualifications rather than indicating his own.

The Kennedy adherents, meanwhile, seemed to be increasingly armed with reasons for supporting his candidacy.

"Did you know he actually *lived* in New York for twenty years?"

"It makes sense that a Democrat will get more out of a Democratic Administration."

"With all those Kennedy millions he ought to be able to help New York."

"He'll have to do a lot for this state if he wants to become President."

"I just like the guy. He's a special kind of person."

The special kind of person assessed his non-debate as a major triumph and continued to chide Senator Keating for barring him from the now-famous Studio 44.

Some reporters, as befits their calling, were skeptical.

"Why did you go down there?" one asked him.

"I just thought that empty chair would look so bad if I didn't go," said a smiling Kennedy.

"You didn't really think you'd get in, did you?"

"I was *sure* I'd get in. I couldn't think of any way they could keep me *out*."

The newsman returned to his typewriter and observed pointedly that the weapon of the old is trickery and the weapon of the young is impulse. Which meant, no doubt, that old Senator Keating's empty-chair trick had been trumped by young Mr. Kennedy's impulsive decision to appear at the studio door.

And so it had.

When Robert Kennedy left the CBS studios he headed for the borough of Queens and three tumultuous rallies. Then at 11 :00 P.M. he was back in Manhattan.

An after-theater crowd of a thousand was waiting for him at a star-spangled rally at the juncture of Broadway and West 53rd Street. Sammy Davis, Jr., Carol Channing, the ubiquitous Shelley Winters, and others cavorted on what was undoubtedly the most modest stage those luminaries had graced in many years—the platform of a spotlighted flat-bed truck.

At one point in the jubilant affair, the candidate took the microphone and joined his friend Sammy Davis in leading a sing-along rendition of "The Sidewalks of New York."

"If things don't go well on November third," concluded Kennedy, "we can go on tour."

Someone in the crowd was reminded of the evening after the President's birthday celebration, when John Kennedy linked arms with Gene Kelly to sing "When Irish Eyes Are Smiling." He had first asked his Vice-President, Lyndon Johnson, to join him and had been told, "I don't sing."

Few would be charitable enough to say that Robert Kennedy did either. But he made a brave try—as he had when he led the Polish folk song "Stolat" in Buffalo and "We Shall Overcome" on the streets of Harlem.

When he finally returned to the Carlyle in the early-morning hours, the attitude of the Kennedy entourage was best summed up by Ed Guthman.

"Things are a lot better," he said.

Five days to election day.

October 28 dawned far brighter than had October 27. At 1:00 P.M., after a crowded morning, Kennedy was scheduled to tape an interview with four Negro leaders at radio station WLIB in Harlem.

I took a cab to the station—I had some papers the candidate would need that afternoon—and arrived several minutes ahead of him. Already there was Andy Hatcher, who was frequently present when Kennedy visited a Negro group. Hatcher had been assistant press secretary to President Kennedy—the first Negro to hold the post—and was now serving his friend Pierre Salinger in his California Senate race.

"How's it going with Pierre?" I asked.

"Fine," said Hatcher confidently. "He hasn't changed his speech since the beginning of the campaign. And it still works fine."

Kennedy arrived to the familiar clamor of children in the streets, taped an interview that dealt almost exclusively with matters of Negro concern, including civil rights, employment, education, and housing, and then returned to his car downstairs.

The weather was extremely mild for this late October day. As the Bonneville wound its way south through Central Park, with the brisk autumn air whipping our faces in the open convertible, Kennedy leafed through the afternoon papers with their reports on the studio encounter of the previous night.

"This Kempton really writes well, doesn't he?" said the candidate.

I looked over his shoulder and read:

> Thus do Lincoln and Douglas come to earth again: Douglas confronting an empty chair and Lincoln confronting three studio guards.

"Nice of him to make you Lincoln," I said.

"I like the last paragraph," said Ed Guthman, leaning over the front seat.

I glanced at the bottom of the column of type.

> You are being asked [wrote Kempton] to choose between an adventurer and a safe man, one who disturbs and one who comforts. These are types suiting different tastes; mine is hopelessly corrupted; my job depends on occasions of high entertainment and I've got to go with the man who comes to play ball.

"Funny," said Kennedy with displeasure, "most of the papers call last night's affair a draw."

"That's just what the papers called the first Kennedy-Nixon debate," I said. "But everyone knew who won it."

"Absolutely right," said Guthman with emphasis. "The papers don't want to tilt it one way or another, so they don't give the edge to anyone. But the people know."

The car pulled up in front of the Carlyle.

"Maybe you're right," said Robert Kennedy.

Two days later, on October 30, with four days remaining before the election, and the respected *Daily News* poll showing him well behind, Senator Kenneth Keating attempted a last-ditch effort to regain the offensive. He purchased a $10,000 hour on NBC television for the following evening and challenged Kennedy to debate him.

The decision was a calculated risk. Some Keating aides opposed it, but the opinion prevailed that Keating had been slipping for weeks, the affair at Studio 44 had been a debacle, morale was crumbling, and Keating must do something to persuade the voters that Kennedy's last-minute appearance was a hoax.

So on the evening of October 30 Senator Kenneth Keating called a press conference and charged that Kennedy, by his "antics" outside the barred studio the previous evening, had "created a false impression." The impression, he said, that Kennedy had been trying to create —evidently with some success—was that Keating was unwilling to debate.

"There is only one way I know of to deal with this matter," said Keating, and more than one reporter must have expected him to produce his card. "I will be at the studio prepared to meet Mr. Kennedy in debate. I have given explicit instructions that NBC officials do nothing to prevent him from entering the studio."

Keating even dropped his last objection in the wrangle over format. He agreed to a Kennedy-Nixon-style debate rather than the classic style on which he had been insisting until then.

Keating then dispatched a telegram to Kennedy in these blunt words:

IF YOU HAVE ANY RESPECT FOR THE JUDGMENT AND INTELLIGENCE OF THE PEOPLE OF NEW YORK YOU WILL MEET ME IN A FACE-TO-FACE DEBATE.

But the calculation failed. Kennedy rejected the offer. His answer was equally blunt:

"My schedule is set. If Mr. Keating wants to come to Rockland or Westchester Counties I'll be glad to debate him there. If not, the Senator does a remarkably good job with an empty chair. He should bring back his empty chair and debate it again."

But this time Kenneth Keating did not debate an empty chair. He debated an empty lectern.

And for added drama during the long hour in which he went through his pantomime of impatient expectation, the camera periodically panned to the studio's open door.

"Here we go again," began the Senator ruefully.

The white-haired legislator insisted that Kennedy had never had any intention of debating the other night but that he "pulled off quite a stunt" by appearing outside the studio door.

"His antics confused the public," conceded Keating, "and that's why I'm here tonight."

At that precise moment Robert Francis Kennedy was aboard a chartered helicopter (rate: $525 per hour) racketing through a suburban campaign circuit. He had departed from the rally at Croton-on-Hudson and was headed for another in Ossining, with two more lying beyond in Tarrytown and at the Rockland County Courthouse.

In the Kennedy press office at the Chatham Hotel, secretaries, speechwriters, researchers, and itinerant newsmen were watching the Keating show on a portable TV set. The Senator was filling the hour with answers to questions phoned in by his viewers.

"This is probably his biggest audience in town," said a reporter.

"I expected another empty chair—with the Senator in it," said a secretary.

"Keep it down," said Bill vandenHeuvel. "I'm phoning in a question."

VandenHeuvel managed to get no less than three questions on the show, which led one to speculate on the size of the Keating audience.

It was a valiant try, but it was not a good show. An hour is far too long to sustain a tone of righteous indignation. And the format was unpalatably dull. Public relations man Tex McCrary would appear every few moments and wordlessly hand a card to the Senator, who would read the question and then undertake to answer it.

In the press office there were some who felt Kennedy should have canceled his suburban rallies to appear on this NBC hour. Their view was that if the CBS nondebate had left a segment of the public in doubt about who did and who didn't wish a debate, Kennedy's absence today would answer that question in a way that was unsatisfactory to the candidate.

But if indeed the Keating forces held a valuable card in Kennedy's absence from the second non-debate, they promptly threw it away a few hours later.

Kennedy was scheduled to be interviewed on the Barry Gray Show, a late-night radio program on which he had appeared earlier in the campaign. The Keating camp learned of this and demanded equal time. Kennedy responded by inviting Keating to *join* him on the program, and Keating accepted.

And with that acceptance, he promptly squandered whatever political capital he could have made of Kennedy's unwillingness to debate him on his $10,000 hour.

The call reached us at the press office. It came from the radio telephone in the candidate's car. Would vanden-Heuvel, Gwirtzman, and I meet him at the offices of WMCA on Madison Avenue—the radio station of the Barry Gray Show—and bring certain documents for reference.

The candidate was speeding back to Manhattan for his date with this much sought after debate, and as usual he would arrive with scarcely time to comb his unruly hair.

When we arrived at 415 Madison Avenue, home of WMCA and site of the Great Debate, we found ourselves in the midst of two noisy battalions of partisans who looked to be about college age. Policemen were laboring mightily to keep the two placard-carrying groups safely separated and finally managed to induce them to picket in two separate circles on the sidewalk.

We waited for the candidate in the ground-floor lobby

as shouts of "We want Keating" and "Kennedy—Kennedy—Kennedy—" split the late-evening air.

Several minutes before eleven o'clock the white-thatched Republican Senator arrived, beaming broadly, and moved through his young admirers into the lobby and onto the elevator. This was the first time in the campaign I had seen him at such close range and I couldn't help feeling a sense of respect and regard for him.

It had been a difficult campaign for Kenneth Keating. His crowds had been dwarfed by the size of his opponent's. He wore the albatross of Goldwater's name at the top of his ticket, yet he could not openly repudiate him. He carried the burden of his sixty-four years through a physically wearing campaign. And his opponent seemed to have an outrageous assortment of high cards: his youth, his vigor, his wealth, his loyalists, and something else that Louis Nizer had seen, when he observed after the empty-chair incident, "What a combination of luck and guts!"

The Barry Gray studio is an attractive place decorated in cool green hues. Its dimensions accommodate with ease the half-dozen guests who normally comprise the guest list on this late-night talk show. But tonight there were somewhat more than a half-dozen.

In the studio itself, along with Gray and his producer, were the two candidates, fourteen photographers, over twenty newsmen from the domestic and foreign press, several Kennedy aides, former Governor Averell Harriman, several Keating aides, campaign manager Herbert Brownell, and Tex McCrary.

That was in the studio proper. In the small control room—stifling hot from the pressure of so many bodies —were more aides, more newsmen, a number of station employees, and four bitterly complaining engineers who kept insisting the show could not go on the air, goddammit, unless they got a little room!

The meeting of the candidates—when Kennedy entered the room a scant few minutes to air time—was correct, if chilly.

"Hello, Bob," said the Senator stiffly.

"Hi, Senator, how are you?" said the challenger.

The two candidates sat flanking Gray at a modernistic table in a flattened-V shape. Kennedy and Keating aides squatted on the floor amidst assorted papers, ready to produce supporting facts as the need arose. Gray's producer, Miss Shelley Andrews, was sprawled on the floor facing Gray and holding a timer to signal the expiration of the answering time. The reporters were seated in five rows of tightly packed seats on one side of the studio. A phalanx of photographers was standing outside the control-room window.

"Just one more, Senator Kennedy," one of them shouted.

"Just a minute," snapped Keating. "He's not in the Senate *yet*."

Kennedy pretended not to hear.

Somebody said, "Fifteen seconds," and the flash bulbs and conversation stopped.

And the debate began.

The format had been agreed upon with surprising ease considering the difficulties that had hobbled all previous negotiations. Each candidate would make an opening and closing statement. Each would answer questions read by Gray and provided by the other's headquarters. Each would have three minutes to answer, and then his adversary would have two minutes for rebuttal.

Kennedy won the toss of a coin and made the first opening statement.

"What this debate is really concerned with," began Robert Kennedy, "is a better future and a better world. My life has been spent in the public service, not for personal reasons, not because of any sacrifice, but because I believe it's the finest thing a man can do. I believe with Lord Tweedsmuir that the public service is the crown of a career, and for a young man the greatest of adventures.

"I do not mean," he continued gently, "to impugn the honesty, sincerity, and integrity of Senator Keating. Senator Keating is a fine gentleman. Our differences are simply that he is a Republican and I am a Democrat and we look at things differently."

Kennedy's statement had been somewhat idealistic and rhetorical. Keating's contrasted sharply. It was vituperative and full of reproach.

"I'm very glad," began the Senator, "to be here face to face with my opponent. It has been a long struggle to get him in a studio with me.

"Within the last ten days there have been published throughout the state and in the papers and in pamphlets the most outrageous distortions of my record. Now, if there were any validity to the distortions of my record that have appeared in these public prints, certainly I would never have received the endorsement of the *New York Times* . . ."

With the opening statements completed, the questioning began. The first one was posed to Kennedy by Keating via Gray, and asked why he had not taken advantage of the opportunity to debate on television earlier that day.

"I made my plans for the last four days," said Kennedy evenly. Then he reviewed the abortive negotiations for a debate, but from a somewhat different perspective than Keating's recital.

The first Kennedy-to-Keating question dealt with the latter's position on the one-man one-vote ruling of the Supreme Court, and the Senator fielded it expertly.

Then Gray coolly recited the next high hard one from the Keating camp: "Mr. Kennedy, the *Reporter* magazine charges you with 'not being above inventing the nonexistent bill or amendment for Senator Keating to have voted against.' How can anyone so careless with the truth pose as a liberal and an idealist?"

The candidate took a deep breath. "Well, all the statements that I've made concerning Senator Keating's record happen to be correct. Now, I would have thought that if Senator Keating's representatives were really interested in the facts they would have brought out a particular bill, a particular vote in which I was wrong. But it is a generalization, accusing me of misstating the facts."

Milt Gwirtzman, sitting on the floor beside him, handed up one of the full-page ads that Senator Keating had been chafing over, and Robert Kennedy proceeded to tick off a string of major measures that Keating had voted to kill, cut, or cripple. As his three minutes ended he was still going strong: "Now, on the Higher Education vote on October 15, 1963—"

"I'm sorry, Mr. Kennedy," said Barry Gray as though he meant it.

Then the Kennedy camp threw a sharp breaking curve.

"Senator Keating," said Gray, "you have been critical of Mr. Kennedy's role in the Philippine–Malaysia–Indonesia dispute. What is your position on an important part of that problem, the dispute between the Philippines and Malaysia over Sabah?"

"The dispute over Sabah?" I whispered to Ed Guthman. "What the hell is Sabah?"

Guthman gave me an enigmatic smile and nothing else.

The Senator struggled through his three minutes, talking about Sukarno and disparaging Kennedy's trip to Indonesia, but never once referring to the Sabah dispute.

"Mr. Kennedy?" said Gray, inviting rebuttal.

"Senator, can I just say that you've accused me continually of distorting your record. And yet when we start talking about specifics, you won't talk about them. You were asked a question about the dispute between Malaysia and the Philippines regarding Sabah. It's extremely important. But, Senator, you never mentioned a word about it in your answer . . ."

Ken Keating hit back hard.

"The *New York Times* has called you 'ruthless in

pursuit of your goals.' Why should the people turn their backs on an outstanding public servant to help you satisfy your personal political ambitions?"

Kennedy paused a moment to gather his thoughts. "Well, Senator," he said with the hint of a smile, "I'll tell you the truth. I don't know that I'm working because I need the money. And I don't need the title or the office space.

"I've been brought up in public service. I started talking about government when I was six years old. It was the only matter, really, that was of great interest to all the members of my family.

"Now, I had to decide what I was going to do after November, 1963, and there were a lot of considerations. I'm thirty-eight years old. I decided that there was unfinished business in the United States. I wanted to be a part of that. And that's why I'm running for the Senate —nothing beyond that."

Finally, as the studio clock stood at 12:18 A.M., the debate ended. Kennedy stood up and reached for Keating's hand. The air of strain and forced cordiality continued to hang over the pale green studio and the Senator still seemed unwilling to meet his opponent's eyes.

Each candidate finally headed for an elevator, trailing his entourage—Keating at the main bank of elevators, Kennedy using those in the rear.

As the elevator door was about to close on us, Barry Gray appeared in the corridor.

"Come on in," said Kennedy. "There's room here."

"Where are you headed?" asked Gray.

"Toots Shor's," said Kennedy.

"I'll meet you there," said Gray.

The atmosphere at the restaurant was festive. We were shown to a table beyond the bar. Averell Harriman was seated beside Maria Cooper, daughter of the late Gary Cooper. Writer Harry Golden was squeezed in between the candidate and Arthur Schlesinger, Jr. Other aides circled the table, and a few minutes after our arrival we somehow managed to make room for Barry Gray and his producer, Shelley Andrews.

"The switchboard is lit up like a Christmas tree," said Miss Andrews.

"We had a tremendous audience tonight," said Barry Gray. "Larger than you would have had on television this afternoon."

"I always knew you had a large audience," said Kennedy. "Everywhere I go in this state there's a group of people shouting, 'We want Barry.' "

At this moment comedian Joe E. Lewis, somewhat in-articulate with drink and smiling warmly, descended on the table to wish the candidate well.

"Joe E. Lewis is going to get sore if he sees this fellow doing that unflattering imitation of him," I whispered to Bill vandenHeuvel.

A few minutes later Toots Shor approached the table, exuding cordiality. "How are you, Senator?" he said in a display of unoriginal commitment. "I'm on my way to a meeting of the Actors Guild. I'll send your regards." And with that the burly restaurateur left to line up the thespian vote.

A short while later Kennedy excused himself, went to a public phone booth near the entrance, and called Glen Cove to tell Ethel how the debate had gone.

"Listen," said Barry Gray, "how about Bob doing my show on *election eve?*"

"Good idea," laughed Harry Golden. "And you could offer Keating equal time the following night."

༺༄

CHAPTER 19

The Next-to-Last Day

The press response to the belated Great Debate was predictably mixed.

The pro-Kennedy *New York Post* editorialized: "The Kennedy-Keating debate effectively brought out the real issue between the two men. It lies less in their respective records than in the contrast between a decent but essentially conventional and uninspired politician and a young leader of great energy and promise."

And said the pro-Keating *New York Herald-Tribune*: "New York needs Senator Keating because he pits the earned respect of his Senatorial colleagues, his knowledge of the ways of the Senate and the necessities of his state, against his opponent's lack of all these qualities."

The partisan claims of victory in the debate were equally predictable.

"Senator Keating indulged in personalities and generalities," Ed Guthman told the press. "Kennedy dealt with facts and the record. We thought Kennedy had the advantage."

Guthman's counterpart at Keating headquarters saw

things somewhat differently: "After Bobby Kennedy's faltering performance, it's understandable why he ran out on two previous debates. Senator Keating was a clear winner on points."

November 1—two days before election day—was a brilliant, sunny day and the candidate seemed relaxed and confident. He refused, however, to concede he was ahead.

The final tabulations of the *Daily News* straw poll showed Kennedy a seven-to-five favorite. Of thirty thousand straws, Kennedy had received seventeen thousand, or 57 percent—Keating had twelve thousand, or 41 percent. The poll showed Kennedy running stronger in New York than his brother had four years before.

But still Robert Kennedy refused to acknowledge an edge, and reporters were busy speculating on the cause of his reluctance. Many Democratic voters, they reasoned, were likely to remain at home on election day due to the impending Johnson landslide. Kennedy would want to make it abundantly clear to his own supporters that he needed their support.

Kennedy's braintrusters acted in a more conventional political manner than their leader. They predicted victory.

Peter Strauss, Kennedy's campaign director, forecast a plurality of over 300,000 votes; the state Democratic chairman, William McKeon, a plurality of 350,000. And former Governor Averell Harriman set the number at a half-million.

Events were to prove them all pessimistic.

• • •

Bob Kennedy spent November 1 campaigning through New York State's southern tier. On this last upstate swing of the campaign, it was necessary to charter a twenty-five-passenger helicopter. Kennedy's targets were seven small towns, and four of them were so small they either had no airport or the landing strips were too small to accommodate the *Caroline*. So, undeterred, the candidate's helicopter set him down in parking lots and ballfields.

A cheerful atmosphere pervaded the Kennedy party. And the only problem one could discern was that of the press in spelling the exotic-sounding names of the counties—Cataraugus, Chanango, Chemung, and Otsego.

Kennedy moved with assurance from town to town, delighted at the size of the crowds that greeted him in these tiny Republican communities where so few politicians ever bothered to venture.

A reporter recalled that during the final days of the Jack Kennedy campaign against Richard Nixon, there was an increasing crackle of levity in his speeches, as his wit flicked his opponent more frequently and more outrageously. In the same way, Robert Kennedy's barbs—more than the prudent election forecasts—seemed to imply his prediction.

In one town the candidate was mobbed by teen-agers and their younger sisters and brothers. Looking out over the sea of young faces, Kennedy said, "You've all heard about FDR being the President of the little people. Well, if I'm elected, I'll be the *Senator* of the little people.

At another stop he said to the youngsters in the crowd, "Back in the last town, I saw a sign that read 'Respectable

Young People for Keating.' Well, I don't know where that leaves you."

The teen-agers laughed, and one of them called out, "There's more of us, Bobby."

At his next stop Kennedy talked about federal aid to education and asked a rhetorical question in the time-honored political way. "When that bill came up for a vote, do you think Senator Keating was on the floor of the Senate?"

"No!" roared the audience.

"Yes, he was," said Kennedy, smiling. "He fought against it and he *voted* against it."

In the tiny town of Cortland, Kennedy spoke from the courthouse steps to an audience that included hundreds of students from Cortland State Teachers College.

"I know about Cortland and about Cortland College," he said, his forefinger stabbing the air. "I wonder whether Ken Keating knows about it. I wonder whether he knows your football team beat East Stroudsberg"— and Kennedy glanced with mock surreptitiousness at a card in his hand—"forty to twenty-four."

The crowds were heavy wherever the candidate went in these upstate counties with the colorful names and the minuscule voting rolls. Seven thousand heard him in Oldan, five thousand in Oneanta, four thousand in Corning, and six thousand in Norwich.

"I say, is six thousand considered a large turnout over here?" asked a correspondent from a London paper.

"It is in Norwich, friend," said a local reporter. "The population is *nine* thousand."

· · ·

Back in New York City, Kenneth Keating was spending the day on a series of television panel shows with such exhortative names as *Searchlight*, *Direct Line*, and *Page One*. Keating's aides, meanwhile, were poring over the depressing figures and forecasts.

Keating's campaign was a paradox. He should have been doing well upstate and poorly in the city. Instead, the traditional alignment had been reversed. His strength was in the city and he was a disappointment in the upstate Republican strongholds. Keating was even doing poorly in his own home town of Rochester.

Kennedy prospects were even stronger than his brother's had been in 1960 in such cities as Buffalo, Syracuse, and Utica. Keating's refusal to endorse Barry Goldwater had maintained his support in New York City, but it had certainly reduced his votes upstate.

In addition, the Conservative Party candidate, a political science professor named Henry Paolucci, though running a generally inept campaign, was cutting into Keating's vote. For even if he only siphoned 50,000 votes from the electorate, these would come out of Keating's column—and this might be critical in a close race.

The main hope of the Keating tactitions was that he could buttress a shaky upstate showing with a strong vote in New York City's suburban counties—Nassau, Suffolk, and Westchester.

But the Kennedy upstate crowds, the predictions of the polls, and the adroitness with which Kennedy had neutralized the principal Keating breakthrough discouraged them.

. . .

During the closing days of the campaign, Robert Kennedy had built up a drumfire of attack on Keating's credentials as a liberal. He had done this through his speeches, statements to the press, television commercials, and advertisements in most of the New York papers.

Keating sought to demonstrate that these attacks were distortions. He recognized that if he could accomplish this, it would strike at the very heart of Kennedy's justification for unseating him, namely, that he had not been vigorous enough in fighting for "liberal" programs.

With a few days remaining in the campaign, Kennedy's advertising agency handed Keating an opportunity to refresh the distortion theme.

They prepared an ad which appeared in several New York newspapers and read: *Adlai Stevenson tells why he's voting for Robert Kennedy. Tonight at 7:25 P.M. on Channel 7.*

A simple, straightforward headline, brief and understated. Except that Adlai Stevenson happened to be a registered voter in Lake County, Illinois, and had already cast his absentee ballot.

"An absolute and utter fabrication," shouted Keating. "This advertising fraud, plus the countless other misrepresentations and distortions by Mr. Kennedy, certainly have earned a public climate by now in which nobody could possibly believe anything Mr. Kennedy might have to say."

The error was what it appeared to be—an exercise in exuberance and rhetorical license by an advertising man.

"It was an agency mistake," said an anguished Fred Papert to the press. "I wrote the copy myself. I just didn't know that Ambassador Stevenson wasn't voting in New York."

The story about the Stevenson ad and Papert's acceptance of responsibility was all over the New York papers, and given the widespread attention the campaign was receiving throughout the country, was on the national tickers as well.

"Relax, Fred," I said to him later that day. "It can't damage Bob. It's obviously an agency mistake."

"Relax, he says," groaned Papert. "All my clients read about how I fouled up the candidate with an inaccurate headline and you say relax."

"But, Fred," I insisted, "you couldn't *buy* this kind of publicity."

CHAPTER 20

The Last Day

At a few minutes to nine on the morning of the last day of the campaign, I arrived at the Kennedy home in Glen Cove.

I found the large game room overflowing with TV cameras, TV cable, admen, cameramen, Kennedy children, nursemaids, aides, men with cue cards, men with Teleprompter rolls, and men whose function was a complete mystery.

A fifteen-minute film was to be produced that morning, rushed to Manhattan for processing, flown to stations across the state, and televised that evening—the night before election day.

Election eve is traditionally the occasion when candidates are at their hearth, their family about them, for the final pleas to the electorate. It is a time when inspiration and idealism replace partisan denunciations. Such a film is what everyone had in mind. But there were certain contrasting opinions.

Fred Papert felt the candidate should speak extemporaneously. Bill Wilson, the agency's TV adviser, felt he should use a script. Lem Billings, Kennedy's friend and advertising adviser, felt the candidate and his children should dress informally. Leland Hayward was for jackets and ties all around. The head cameraman warned dourly that unless the film was completed by noon it could not be processed in time to reach the upstate stations. And on and on and on . . .

Time ticked away and when 10:00 A.M. arrived the candidate was still not in evidence.

I looked morosely out the dining-room window and observed three young Kennedys gamboling across the lawn. If their father arrived this very minute, I thought, there would still be the delay in changing them into the clothes that I was sure he would feel were suitable.

I told a housekeeper to ask Mrs. Robert Kennedy if I could see her. A few moments later the woman reappeared on the green-carpeted staircase and said that Mrs. Kennedy was available. I followed her up the steps, down a quiet corridor, and into a large, comfortably furnished bedroom. Seated in the middle of the room, with much of her head concealed in an electric dryer, was Ethel Kennedy.

"Hi," she said.

"Hello," I said.

"What was that?"

"I said *hello*."

"You'll have to speak a little louder. I can't hear a thing with this dryer."

"It's about the *children's clothes*." I shouted.

"Yes?"

"I think they should be in jackets and ties."

[*178*]

"The girls too?" said Ethel, smiling.

"Yes, especially the girls," I said. "No, really. There's some dispute about it belowstairs, and since we're so short on time, I thought we ought to resolve it now."

"We ought to what?"

"*Resolve it now*," I said.

"I think you're right," said Ethel Kennedy just as her husband came into the room and scooped up sixteen-month-old Christopher in his arms.

"Hi," said the candidate.

"We're all set," I said rather superfluously.

"Good," said the candidate. He walked down the corridor and into one of the children's bedrooms, planting a kiss on Kerry's blond locks and mussing David's hair.

A few moments later the candidate strode back into the master bedroom. Ethel had been extricated from the dryer and was applying some make-up at the dressing-table mirror.

"Nearly ready?" said Kennedy.

"Just another minute," said Ethel, applying a last touch of eye shadow.

"As pretty as the day he married you," I said.

"Sure," said Ethel Kennedy. "But now it takes longer."

As Mr. and Mrs. Robert Kennedy entered their game room, they looked about at the mass of television cable, cameras, and equipment, and the dozens of people milling about.

"Well, here we are," said Ethel, "just an average American family."

Leland Hayward greeted the Kennedys in the charming manner which enabled him to deal so effectively with Broadway's most famous unmanageables. "If you'll just get all the children together—" he said in a tone that suggested it would be like assembling the Normandy invasion force.

The children were everywhere—on the lawn, at the pool, upstairs being changed. But soon the entire family, save little Christopher, the Kennedys' infant, was seated on the two large sofas that formed a V at the fireplace. Christopher was being held by a nursemaid and would be placed in the picture just before the cameras churned. The strategy then called for the camera to pan to a close shot of the candidate while Christopher would be urged—with soundless gestures from behind the cameras—to come toddling noiselessly but promptly out of the scene. It seemed a hazardous enterprise, but no one could suggest a workable alternative.

"Now let's just arrange the children into a nice composition," said Hayward.

We've got the right man, I thought. Anyone who could manage all those children in *The Sound of Music* can certainly carry *this* off.

"All right, that's fine," said Hayward, peering judiciously at the scene through the television camera. "Let's film it. Since we don't have time for editing the different pieces, we'll have to shoot the whole fifteen minutes all at once. All right, let's go."

Christopher was deposited in his mother's lap, the cameras turned, and the candidate began to speak.

"Good evening," he said. "It's good to be home. I'd

like you to meet my family." The camera began its slow pan. "My wife, Ethel . . . my daughter Kathleen . . . my sons Joe . . . and Bobby . . . *Wait* a minute. You're David, aren't you?"

The children giggled, the cameramen smiled, and the candidate continued. "Courtney . . . Michael . . . Kerry . . . and Christopher."

The camera panned back to the candidate and Ethel Kennedy deposited little Christopher on the floor. As his nursemaid gestured wildly from the side of the room, and cameramen and technicians sent up a prayer, Christopher began to toddle toward his nursemaid. After several false starts in which he threatened to wander back into the focus of the camera, Christopher reached protective arms and a great sigh went up around the room.

"Over the past few weeks," said Robert Francis Kennedy, abandoning the Teleprompter and speaking extemporaneously, "I've been traveling about the State of New York and you've given me a very warm welcome. And I appreciate that.

"As I've traveled about, I've tried to talk about the great issues that face us—the great problems and the great opportunities—and what I feel are, basically, our responsibilities.

"Our responsibility to our young people, for example, for a good education and a decent atmosphere in which to grow up.

"Our responsibility to our elderly who've given so much to our society in our lifetime.

"Our responsibility to those who are less fortunate than we are—the hungry and the needy and the jobless.

"And, basically, our responsibility to ourselves—to live up to our society—to make a contribution—to use what gifts we have to move our country a little further along and make it a better place to live.

"And now this campaign is over and tomorrow the people will decide. But today on election eve, I'm at home and I can't help thinking what a very exciting campaign it has been. Certain things stand out in my memory, and I thought you might enjoy watching with us some of the moments that have made it such a memorable experience for me."

At this point a TV monitor began to show a series of film clips from the campaign, and the candidate's voice moved in deftly to provide the commentary.

There was the candidate standing on the hood of a car moving slowly down a Harlem street, tossing a football back and forth to the teen-agers who trotted ahead of his car . . .

There was the candidate stooping to pull up the socks of his son David before they started up Fifth Avenue in the Columbus Day parade . . .

There was the candidate stepping through the door of a farmhouse, holding a jug of cider over his shoulder and taking a long pull . . .

There was the candidate, bareheaded in a rainstorm, addressing a thick forest of umbrellas . . .

There was Kennedy being dragged from the rear deck of a car by overaffectionate fans . . . Kennedy mobbed at the beach . . . Kennedy mobbed in the theater district . . . Kennedy mobbed and mobbed again . . .

During the candidate's introductory remarks, as he

talked of our responsibilities to the young and the old, Ed Guthman had peered through the camera lens and noticed that daughter Courtney was mugging outrageously and that her face was quite visible in the television frame.

"That's no good," whispered Guthman. "We ought to stop it and start over."

"Can't do it," said the head cameraman, and the film rolled on.

After Kennedy's final remarks the filming ended. The children heaved a sigh of freedom and went racing for the out-of-doors. The candidate and his wife arose with an expression of evident relief. And Leland Hayward, aware of Courtney's mugging, walked up to Robert Kennedy and performed an act of great moral courage.

"Wonderful," said Hayward. "A really wonderful rehearsal."

"*What?*" exploded Kennedy.

"Now let's do the final print. You needed one good run-through."

Kennedy was controlling his temper with difficulty. "Do you think these children are going to sit through another fifteen minutes?" And without waiting for an answer, he marched through the door, onto the patio, and across the back lawn, heading for the horizon.

A strategy meeting was called at the highest level. It was decided that the film must be redone, since Courtney's antics had rendered this version less than satisfactory. But to spare the children fifteen more tortured minutes of silence and immobility, we thought the candidate should ask them to leave after the segment of film clips.

Leland Hayward walked out across the lawn to where Robert Kennedy was standing deep in thought. "I'm sorry about the strain on the children, Bob," he said. "But the agency felt that you needed at least one run-through as a dress rehearsal."

"Then the agency doesn't know a thing about children," said Kennedy flatly.

Hayward explained the alternative he had worked out, the candidate agreed, and the children were rounded up again from the four corners of the estate. Little Christopher was held in readiness.

My wristwatch read 11:35 A.M. This "take" would have to be good if we were to meet the noon deadline.

Once again the cameras churned. And this time the candidate's performance was better than before. After the segment of news film ended, he did not dismiss the children as we had planned—they were beautifully behaved and not showing any sign of restlessness.

And Courtney had been situated safely out of camera range at the far end of the couch, where all through the film she was mugging outrageously.

The film was completed and the agency men dispatched it to Manhattan for processing, duplication, and shipment to TV stations around the state. The candidate thanked the technicians and left for a series of afternoon rallies.

Leland Hayward stood in the entrance to the game room and surveyed the complicated lighting equipment, the cameramen packing their gear, the advertising men packing their attaché cases, the cue cards strewn about, the nursemaids and toddlers and children and secretaries.

"You know," said Hayward, "this would make the goddamndest musical comedy the Broadway stage has ever seen." And with that he walked out of the room.

CHAPTER 21

><

The End of It

Robert Kennedy rose on November 3 to learn whether his career in politics was ending or beginning.

Election day was a leisurely day by Kennedy standards. He was up before dawn to breakfast with members of the West Side Democratic Club, then visited his headquarters on 42nd Street to thank the youthful staff for their efforts.

And then he was off to the Bronx Zoo with Ethel and the children.

It is said that George Jessel loved to visit the zoo, for after the animals were fed he would make a speech. There was neither opportunity nor precedent for making a speech on this brisk, sunny election day. So the candidate satisfied himself by purchasing bags of unshelled peanuts for his children.

"Please do not feed the candidate," said Ethel impishly.

Before the elephant's cage, four-year-old Kerry Kennedy extended a handful of peanuts through the bars. A long trunk unwound itself and gently lifted them from her hand. Kerry was delighted with this heady experience, and in a fit of joy, seized her father and kissed him ferociously on the cheek.

"Please, Kerry," laughed the candidate, "I told you—only when there are cameramen around!"

The Stephen Smiths have a duplex apartment at 950 Fifth Avenue. When the cab bearing my wife and me arrived there at nine-thirty that evening we found a cluster of policemen at the door being studiously ignored by the doorman.

As the elevator carried us upward, I recalled my reaction when, the day before, I had seen the guest list for this election-night party. It read like a *Who's Who* of politics and the arts. The list embraced the theater, the world of books, government, music, motion pictures, and high society.

Well, I thought, the Kennedys always did throw extraordinary parties.

It suddenly occurred to me that had Jack Kennedy lived and run for re-election, that would undoubtedly have been one of the kinds of vilification he would have suffered in a bruising Presidential campaign.

"They're more interested in fancy parties than in ordinary folks." So the line would have run.

It had seemed to me that much of the abuse heaped upon Robert Kennedy during the campaign came from those who bitterly resented the secure place his brother now held in America's affections. Jack Kennedy was beyond their vilification. But there was always Bobby . . .

I realized with a chilling sense of irony that today tributes to John Kennedy flow from a thousand sources and his legend grows daily. But had he lived to run again, he would have been subjected to the same hate and calumny that was aimed at his brother all through those long autumn months.

The elevator opened into a small hall leading to a large living room that was alive with people.

As we left the elevator, Averell Harriman entered it, struggling into his coat. Four of the Kennedy children were also donning hats and coats preparing to follow their parents who, we later learned, had left for the Statler-Hilton a few minutes earlier.

Sitting on the living-room floor, her legs curled up beneath her, was Jacqueline Kennedy. She sat facing a TV set in the corner which was spewing facts, most of them unintelligible, over the general din in the room.

Beside Mrs. Kennedy was Washington columnist Rowland Evans and British Ambassador David Ormsby-Gore.

Standing in the corner, deep in conversation, were Jean Kennedy Smith, Arthur Schlesinger, James Wechsler, and a Kennedy cousin, Polly Fitzgerald.

We walked through the French doors and into a high-ceilinged den furnished in the pale shades of nineteenth-century Empire. On a love seat were Peter Lawford and Piedy Gimbel, looking removed from the agitation on the other side of the doors.

Through the living room's other door was the dining room, and seated at a table were Leland Hayward, Pamela Churchill Hayward, and Mrs. Rose Kennedy—

the woman Adlai Stevenson had called "the head of the most successful employment agency in America." She was blue-eyed and smiling, and I recalled the first time I had met her.

The candidate, his wife, and I were on our way to a speaking engagement at a midtown hotel. We had stopped on a street in the East Seventies, and there on the sidewalk was Mrs. Joseph Kennedy, standing behind a wheelchair in which sat her husband. She told her third son about what she had been doing in his behalf and what her plans were for the next few days. And the words tumbled out excitedly. John Kennedy had called her "the best politician in the family," and she was doing her best.

When we bade them goodnight and climbed back in the car, Bob Kennedy turned to me and said, "How old do you think my mother is?"

I said I didn't know.

"She's seventy-three. Isn't that amazing?"

Mrs. Jacqueline Kennedy entered the room.

"How do things look?" said Mrs. Hayward.

"Oh, they look quite good," she said. "But I don't see why Bob doesn't make a statement."

"I don't think he'd want to do that until Keating concedes," said Hayward.

"I don't know. Isn't there someone you can call at NBC, Leland?"

Hayward sensed there was no purpose in phoning the network, but to placate Mrs. Kennedy he left the room and dialed the home number of Ed Friendly, a top NBC executive. He returned a few moments later.

"There's no answer," said Hayward.

"Well," said Jacqueline Kennedy, "thanks for trying."

"CBS has given the election to Bobby," someone called from the living room.

"They did *that*," said Hayward, "before there was a vote on the board."

We returned to the living room and found a mass exodus under way. Everyone was now anxious to get over to the Statler-Hilton, and I estimated there were at least two carfuls of people backed up at the elevator door.

"Let's walk down," said Peter Lawford.

He led the way through the host of servants in the large kitchen, and down the back stairs. It was three long flights—an especially challenging romp for the ladies in their high heels—and when we reached the bottom we found a fire door. It was locked and held securely by a reinforced rubber chain.

The group started back up the stairs.

"Wait a minute," said Lawford, and reared back to smash his foot against the door. He kicked it again and again, but still the chain held.

He gave it one final kick and exploded in a mild obscenity. Then he looked up and saw a lady on the landing above him. "Oh, excuse me," he said.

We retraced our steps up the stairs. Providentially, two flights up we came upon a freight elevator that yawned open and we entered it.

"Had a little accident in the guest elevator coming down from the Smiths'," said the driver.

"What sort of accident?" snapped Lawford.

"Cable broke and it fell to the basement."

"Good Lord!" said Lawford.

"Nobody injured," said the man laconically.

Down in the street we piled into Lawford's big black limousine and were driven to the Statler-Hilton, in whose main ballroom the Kennedy faithful were gathered.

We went to the hotel's tenth floor and found the corridor crowded with Kennedy partisans for over a hundred yards of its length.

The corridor ended in the door to a spacious suite reserved for the inner circle. It was the most numerous inner circle you ever saw. Among them was Fred Papert, fully recovered from his literary excess in the Adlai Stevenson ad. There was Lem Billings, looking animated, and Angie Novello, looking pleased.

And there was Barry Gray, looking stunned.

Gray had the distinction of being a loser on the day *before* election day. In an election-eve interview with a Keating aide on his late-night interview show, Gray had, according to his employers, "failed to adhere to the station's standards of fair play." The Keating man had brought up Kennedy's role as council to the late Senator McCarthy's subcommittee. Gray had rasped, "You have an oily way about you, sir."

Gray had been promptly suspended.

His conduct on election eve was in sharp contrast to his scrupulously impartial behavior on the Kennedy-Keating debate which he moderated before those same microphones a few evenings before. But spirits were running high, and Gray's abrasive tongue was the element that gave his program its controversial flavor and its wide following.

"If you could just break yourself of expressing opinions, Barry, you could lose your audience overnight," I said.

"I could have used better words," said Gray. "I think I may have lost my temper." And he drifted off in search of a drink.

We moved deeper into the room, and there, surrounded by a brood of seven children who sat or squatted and stared fixedly at a television set, we found Ethel Kennedy.

"I expected to see you back at the apartment," I said.

"We left in kind of a hurry," said Ethel. "We had just come to the beef Stroganoff when Bobby said he wasn't getting the returns fast enough and he ought to be with his people. He said, 'Get in the elevator,' and here we are."

On the television screen we observed that Keating was also with his people. There he stood, smiling up into the punishing television lights and surrounded by his supporters in the ballroom of the Roosevelt Hotel. These people had a smart country-club look that made the lusty outcries of the Kennedy partisans seem in slightly bad taste. "I sure hope I don't let you down," Keating said.

"There's no character in his face," said a woman behind me. "Bobby has those wonderful sad eyes—"

"Look at Keating's eyes later tonight," said her companion.

I pushed my way through the crowd to a door that opened on a two-room suite in which the candidate, the rest of his family, and his aides were watching the returns.

Standing in the center of the room, staring down at the TV, was Robert Kennedy. Behind him, on a pair of bridge chairs, were sisters Eunice Kennedy Shriver and Jean Kennedy Smith.

Off to the right, sunken deep in a club chair, was Dorothy Kilgallen, who observed in her column the next day that in this inner chamber Bob Kennedy was surrounded by a curious mélange of people, "from both uptown and downtown."

Bernie Ruggieri, Mayor Wagner's political adviser, was listening on the phone and scribbling numbers on a small blue pad.

"That sounds good," he said shortly, tore off the page, and handed it to the candidate.

Barry Gray ambled into the room. The candidate saw him and crossed to him at once.

"What happened to you?" said Kennedy with a mixture of concern and astonishment.

"Don't ask!" said Gray rhetorically, and led him over to the corner to tell him of the pains his commitment had earned him.

Finally Kennedy returned to the set.

"Here are some notes for a victory statement," said Bill vandenHeuvel, handing him a sheet of paper.

His eyes gulped it down. "Yes," he said somewhat abstractedly. "Let's go inside where we can talk." He led the way into the bedroom.

"I think," said Kennedy, "the statement should include my belief that America should not be deprived of the services of such a dedicated public servant as Senator Keating."

"Shouldn't you add," said vandenHeuvel, "that you will do whatever you can to facilitate that?"

Kennedy thought a moment. "No, I think that might sound patronizing."

"What about this quote from Tennyson—" began Gwirtzman, but suddenly a commotion had begun in the room from which we had come. It was just 12:40 A.M.

"Keating's going to make a statement," called Eunice Shriver, and the room filled with applause.

The candidate strode into the living room and stood facing the set, his arms crossed, his face intent. Suddenly the room was very quiet as the white-haired Senator prepared to make his concession statement and the youthful candidate stood staring earnestly at the screen.

When his followers had finally grown quiet, Senator Kenneth Keating slowly began to read a telegram which he was dispatching to his opponent. "Dear Bob," he read. "I congratulate you on your victory—"

There were shouts from the crowd surrounding the Senator. No doubt such proclamations always produce the bitter, incredulous cries of "No, no!" But Keating ignored them.

"The people of New York," he continued, "have expressed their judgment. I stand ready to help you in any way I can—"

Senator Jacob Javits and Governor Nelson Rockefeller stared somberly over Keating's shoulder. This had been a damaging night for them and a damaging campaign.

The banner of moderate Republicanism had suffered eclipse and humiliation and now a most devastating defeat.

"These have been six rewarding years in the United States Senate—" said Kenneth Keating.

Robert Kennedy stared soberly at the screen and the look on his face was not one of triumph.

Keating concluded his remarks and then Nelson Rockefeller made his. They were somewhat ungracious. The Governor said that the State of New York had suffered a grievous blow this day with the defeat of Kenneth Keating and the election of Robert Kennedy.

A smile broke over Kennedy's face. "I was beginning to feel bad," he said.

Suddenly a phone near the window was ringing. Barry Gray was one of a knot of people around it and picked it up.

"It's for you, Bob," said Gray in a peculiarly wooden voice.

"Who is it?" said Kennedy.

"It's the President," said Gray.

There was a bit of scurrying about as the call was transferred into the bedroom so the Senator-elect could receive the congratulations of the Commander in Chief in some privacy.

When Robert Kennedy emerged from the room again he walked into the outstretched arms of a handsome woman with a husky voice.

"Congratulations," said Marlene Dietrich as she kissed him in a most ungrandmotherly way.

The phone was jangling again and Ed Guthman took the call.

"It's Bob McNamara," he said.

"He's calling to say that as a new economy move he's shutting down the Senate," said vandenHeuvel.

The candidate spoke to the Secretary of Defense. Then he left the suite and walked slowly through the crowds of well-wishers that lined the corridor, heading for the grand ballroom where he would make his victory statement to the TV cameras and the party faithful.

The most closely watched, most tenaciously fought Senate campaign in America had ended. Robert Kennedy was the Senator-elect from the State of New York.

The torch had been passed.

CHAPTER 22

The Beginning

From the Statler-Hilton we proceeded to a victory celebration at Delmonico's on Park Avenue at 59th Street.

The elegant restaurant was alive with excitement. Two television sets flanked the small stage and each was the focus of a knot of people intently watching the Johnson landslide roar in. And they were also watching the California race. For Pierre Salinger, late of the New Frontier, was in deep trouble.

His friend and long-time aide, Andy Hatcher, watched one of the sets and his face was full of distress.

"How's he doing?" I asked.

"It's all right," he said in a tone that belied the words. "It's all right. I'm going to call him now. It's going to be all right." And with that he darted off.

On the bandstand, Richard Adler, the composer of *The Pajama Game* and *Damn Yankees*, was at the microphone. He was clearly nettled at the inattention of his audience.

Adler had found his way into the Kennedy circle through poll-taker Lou Harris and had nearly wiped out the Democratic debt single-handed by producing a mammoth fund-raising show at Madison Square Garden on Jack Kennedy's forty-fifth birthday.

"Marilyn Monroe broke her contract to come to New York and sing 'Happy Birthday,' he told me. "She showed me how she planned to do it and I was sick with fear. It was so—sexy. I called up the President, and Kennedy said he didn't see why I was so upset. 'Sing it to me the way she's going to do it,' he said. So I did, and Kennedy roared. He said, 'I think my political career will survive it.' "

Now Richard Adler was facing his Delmonico's audience with obvious annoyance. "Ladies and gentlemen," he said, "we have some exciting entertainment for you tonight. I'd like to present to you—Mr. Tony Bennett."

Tony Bennett undoubtedly had many admirers in the room. Yet sad to say, no one paid very much attention. He sang a rhythm tune and a ballad and then he retired from the scene after what must rank as the most unsuccessful benefit performance in history.

Adler again mounted the bandstand as though it were a Korean hill. By now his petulance was turning to malice. I would have hated to see him if Kennedy *lost*.

"And now if we can *please* have some quiet, I'd like to present to you the man who is perhaps the greatest entertainer of them all—Mr. Sammy Davis, Jr."

A slight figure wearing a skin-tight suit moved among the tables and up onto the stage. It is a tribute to the talent of Sammy Davis that after the first eight bars, the conversation in the room, if it did not quite evaporate, at least grew muffled.

Davis was the last of the entertainment—or perhaps just the last who would brave the massive indifference of the crowd.

Then suddenly Robert Kennedy entered the restaurant.

As he moved among the tables, touching a shoulder here, smiling at someone there, offering the tentative wave, it seemed to me that never in all the days of the campaign had Robert Kennedy appeared so out of place as he did in the casual atmosphere of this club.

Perhaps it was because the battle was over and this was a time and place for relaxation, for small talk, for frivolity.

And then I recalled Robert Kennedy on another occasion speaking of the social circuit and saying, "Nobody who goes to those things all the time makes any real contribution."

At three-thirty in the morning Senator-elect Kennedy left Delmonico's and returned to the spot where his turbulent campaign had begun nine weeks before—the Fulton Fish Market.

Horns blared as the Kennedy motorcade started its last journey along the redolent cobblestones of South Street. Men crowded around him, urging fish upon him as they had that early September morning that now seemed so long ago.

"I voted for you, Bobby!" a workman shouted.

Another grabbed him and kissed him unashamedly on the cheek.

Leaving the Fulton Market, Kennedy enjoyed a few

fleeting hours of sleep and then embarked on yet another sentimental journey—he flew to Glens Falls.

As he climbed up the ramp, Terry Smith of the *Tribune* caught his eye.

"Well, it's all over," said Smith.

"Yes, now I can go back to being ruthless." Kennedy laughed.

Glens Falls was the place where a third of a town had waited in the darkness for five hours to greet him— women in nightgowns and children in pajamas, they waited. So the day after the election Robert Kennedy returned to Glens Falls as he had promised. And this time he brought his wife.

"I appreciate your waiting for Bobby that day," said Ethel Kennedy to the crowd. "When he got home, he told me about it. You all looked very nice in your pajamas."

Then the Kennedys left for Boston for a date with Ted Kennedy, who was still recuperating from his back injury. Ted had also been a winner.

It had been quite a day. Now there were three Kennedy brothers who had been elected to the United States Senate. It did not seem a record that would soon be matched. And no one could reasonably predict how many other records this extraordinary family was yet to set.

As the *Caroline* carried Robert Kennedy toward Boston, his plurality continued to rise. When the last vote was counted it would be over 700,000.

The Kennedys, as James Reston once observed, seldom picked the easy fights. The job of unseating Senator Kenneth Keating—especially for a young man with a Boston accent—was *going* to be rough. That was the Kennedy way. You bit off more than you could chew. And then you chewed it.

Kennedy had done it in part by exploiting his opponent's errors. And by keeping his own to a minimum. He worked hard and was not afraid to take some dangerous risks when events required them.

He organized his campaign with the same thoroughness that had characterized his older brother's campaign in 1960.

He developed rapidly into a good stump speaker with an unerring feeling for the most persuasive points. And he displayed his dry Irish wit to good advantage.

He surrounded himself with a group of effective people and earned their loyalty by his own sincerity, hard work, and unfailing civility.

He convinced the voters that he would "make a difference"—that he would be a vigorous Senator who could do more for the state.

Robert Kennedy trailed Lyndon Johnson by nearly a million votes, and some of his detractors called it a coat-tail victory. But that was hardly the case. Bob Kennedy surpassed by nearly 400,000 votes the plurality his brother John had piled up in New York four years before.

Indeed, if a Johnson landslide was enough to assure a coat-tail victory, then Pierre Salinger was the victim of some grave conspiracy.

So now it was over.

And as it always seemed to be with the Kennedys, where one road ended, another began.

The end of the affair is the beginning of the next.

"I believe," he had said to the throng at the Statler-Hilton, "I believe this vote is a mandate to continue the efforts begun by my brother four years ago—the effort to get something started in this country."

And having said that, Robert Francis Kennedy set out on a New Frontier of his own.

ABOUT THE AUTHOR

GERALD GARDNER

is perhaps best known for his varied contributions to the recent trend of political satire. He is the author of Who's in Charge Here?, *a million-copy best seller, and chief writer and co-creator of the American television program* That Was the Week That Was. *He is the author of* The Quotable Mr. Kennedy, *and with cartoonist Frank Johnson, created Miss Caroline, a syndicated newspaper feature. He is also the author of* The Shining Moments, *a tribute to the late President Kennedy. Other books by Mr. Gardner include* Looks Like a Landslide, News Reals, *its sequel* New News Reals, *and* Is That Seat Taken?, *a volume about the cinema. He is a contributor to the* New York Times Book Review, Playboy, TV Guide *and* Mad, *and writes a monthly column for* Saga *magazine. A book of his satiric songs has recently been published under the title* These Are the Songs That Were.

Mr. Gardner served as Robert Kennedy's aide and speechwriter during his campaign for the U.S. Senate and chronicled his experiences in this volume. He is a native New Yorker, is married—his wife, Harriet, is also a writer—and has two children, Lindsay and Joanna. The Gardners divide their time between their homes in Oradell, New Jersey, and Beverly Hills, California.